Lillenas

I WILL SING OF MY

Redeemer

Medium Voice Solos for Special Occasions

Compiled and Arranged by Marty Parks

I Call Him Lord

Words and Music by
DOTTIE RAMBO
Arranged by Marty Parks

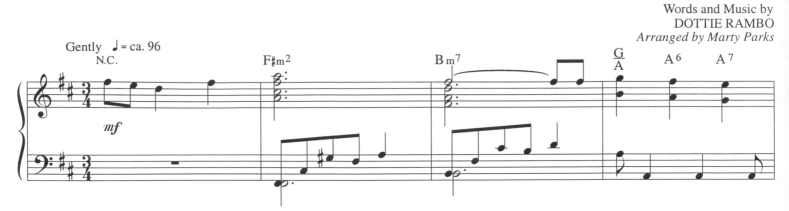

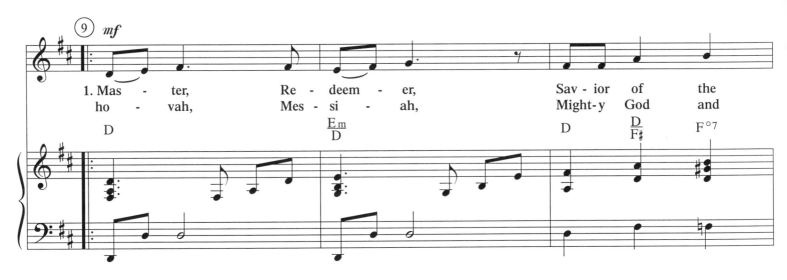

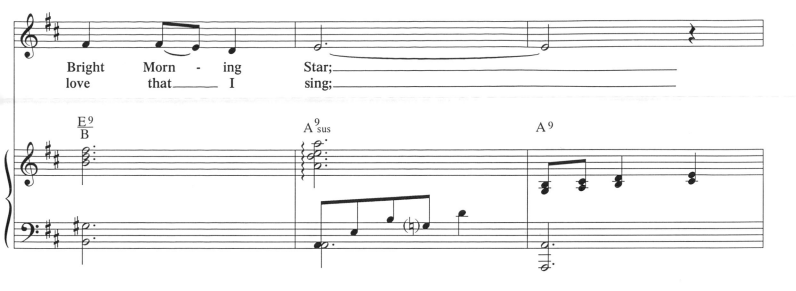

Bright Morn - ing Star;
love that I sing;

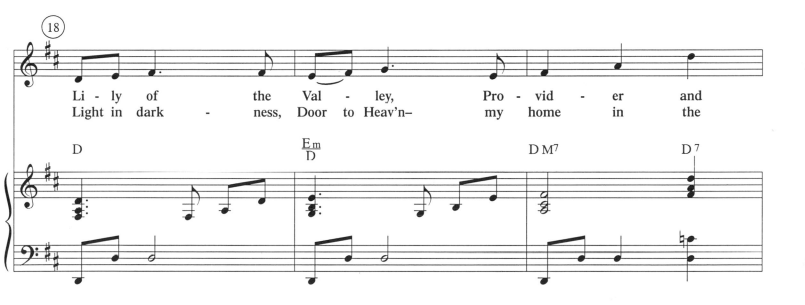

Li - ly of the Val - ley, Pro - vid - er and
Light in dark - ness, Door to Heav'n– my home in the

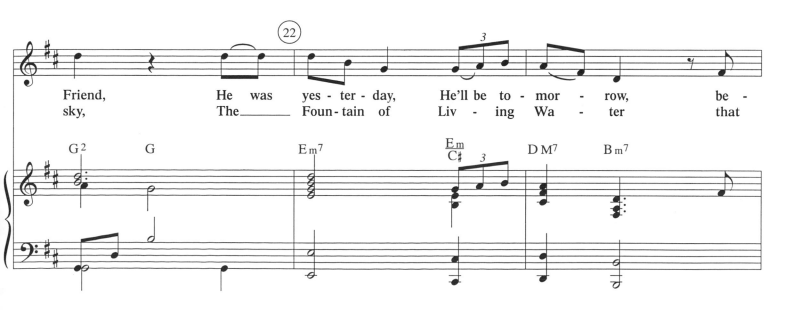

Friend, He was yes - ter - day, He'll be to - mor - row, be -
sky, The Foun - tain of Liv - ing Wa - ter that

gin - ning and end._____

nev - er shall run dry._____ And the

Em7 A6 A7 D

rit. ㉘ a tempo

an - gel called Him Je - sus,

GM7/A D2 D

Born of a_____ vir - gin;

G/D A/D G/D D2 D

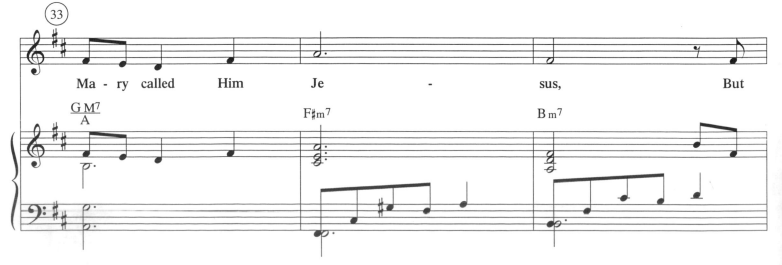

㉝

Ma - ry called Him Je - sus, But

GM7/A F#m7 Bm7

I call Him Lord.

(to pg. 2, meas. 9)

2. Je - Lord.

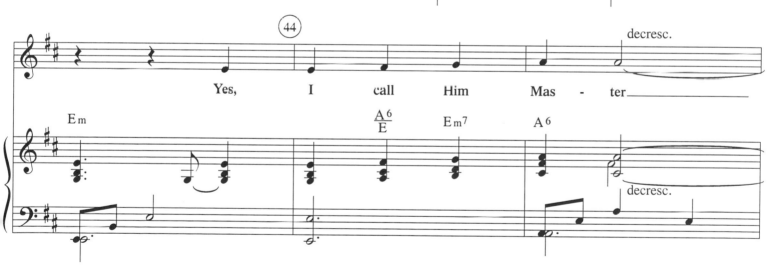

Yes, I call Him Mas - ter

decresc.

and Lord.

mp

rit.

The Lamb of Christmas

KEN BIBLE

French Melody, 13th Century
Arranged by Marty Parks

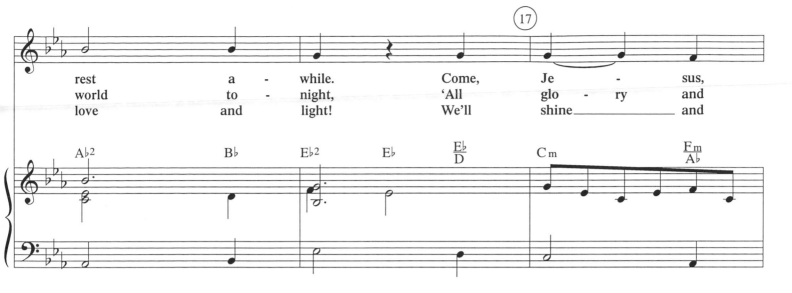

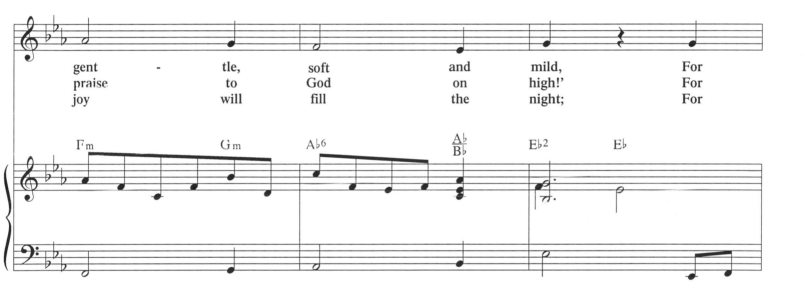

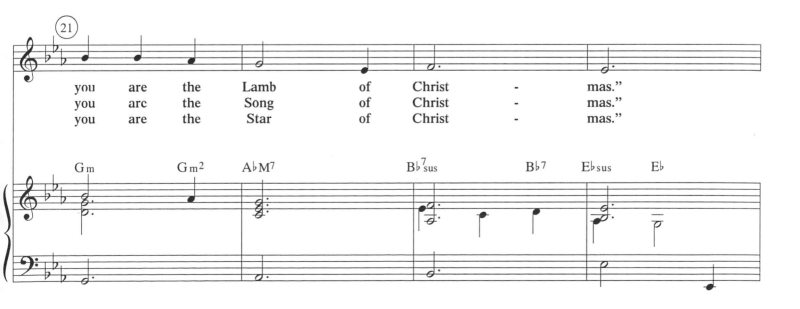

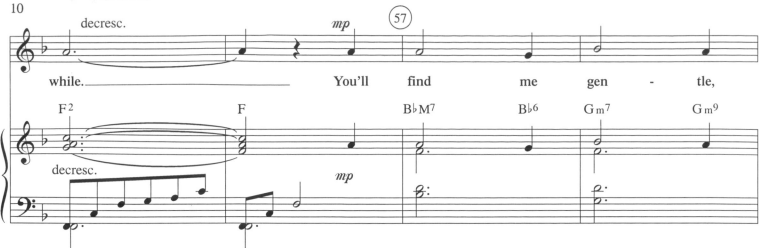

while._____ You'll find me gen - tle,

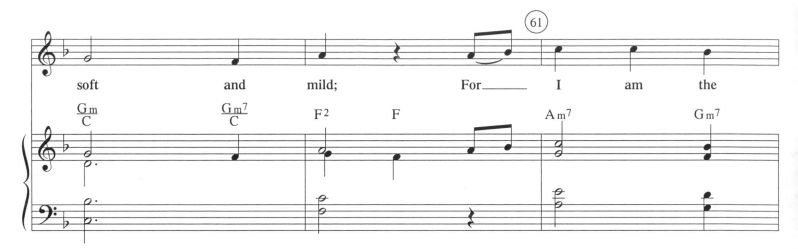

soft and mild; For_____ I am the

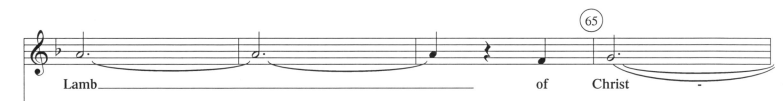

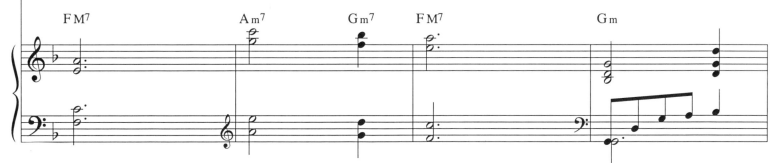

Lamb_____ of Christ -

- mas."_____

Jesus

(Jesu, Joy of Man's Desiring)

KEN BIBLE

JOHANN SCHOP
Adapted by J.S. Bach
arranged by Marty Parks

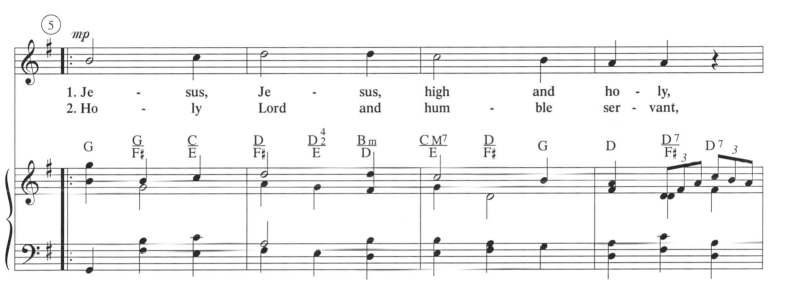

1. Je - sus, Je - sus, high and ho - ly,
2. Ho - ly Je Lord and hum - ble ser - vant,

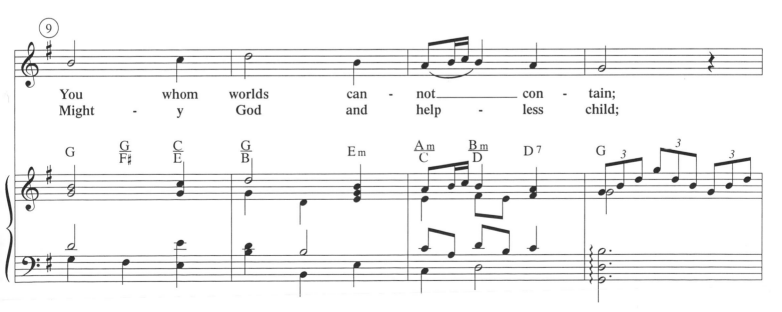

You whom worlds can - not con - tain;
Might - y God and help - less child;

*In measure 23, the cued note "B" may be sung on beats 1 and 2 for a less ornamented rendition.

(to pg. 11, meas. 5)

*In measure 27, the cued note "D" may be sung on beats 1 and 2 for a less ornamented rendition.

O Little Town of Bethlehem

with
Once In Royal David's City

PHILLIPS BROOKS

Traditional English Melody
Arranged by Marty Parks

*"Once in Royal David's City"

Where a moth-er laid her Ba-by in a man-ger for His bed;

Db   Ab/Db   Gb/Db   Db   Bbm   Bbm/Ab   Gb   Ab7   Db

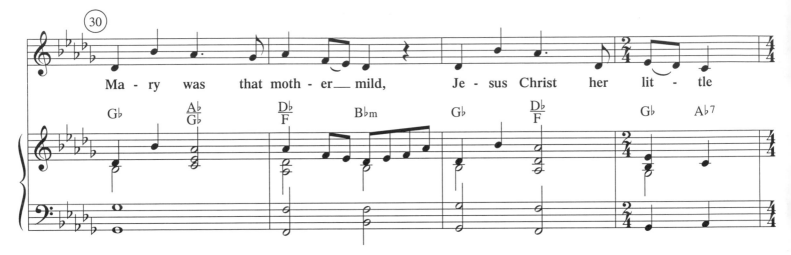

Ma-ry was that moth-er mild, Je-sus Christ her lit-tle

Gb   Ab/Gb   Db/F   Bbm   Gb   Db/F   Gb   Ab7

Child.   For Christ is born of Ma-ry, and,

Db   Bbm   Bbm6/G   Csus   C   F   Bb   F/A   Gm/Bb   F   Dm   C   D/F#

gath-ered all a-bove,   While mor-tals sleep, the

Gm   F/A   Bb6   C7   Fsus   F   F   Bb   F/A   Gm/Bb

At the Right Time

Words and Music by
MOSIE LISTER
Arranged by Marty Parks

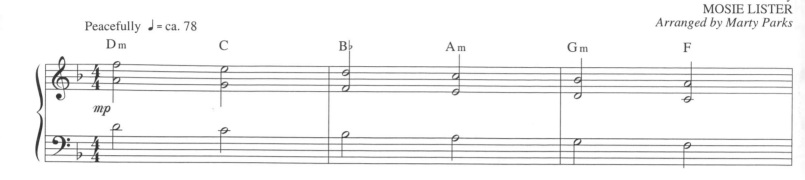

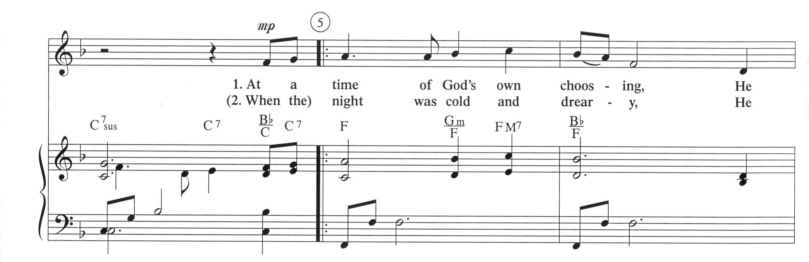

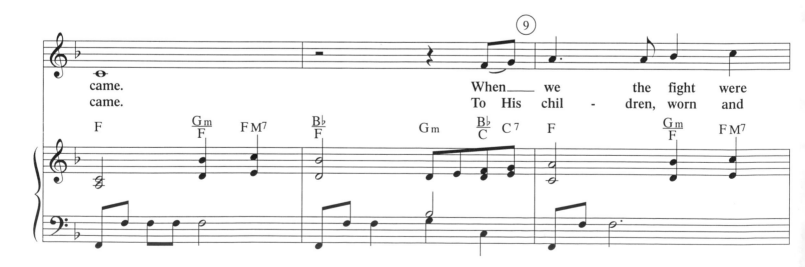

Immanuel

Words and Music by
MICHAEL CARD
Arranged by Marty Parks

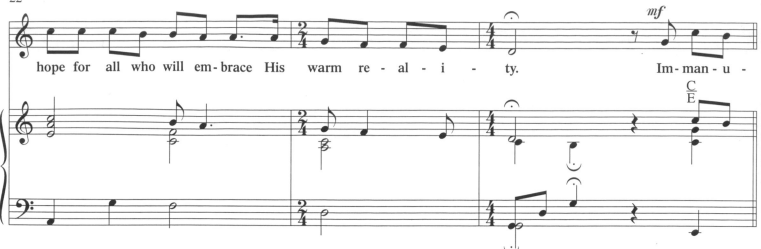

hope for all who will em-brace His warm re-al-i-ty. Im-man-u-

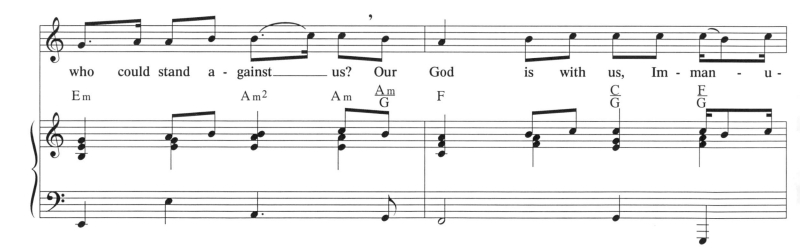

el, Our God is with us, And if God is with us,

who could stand a-gainst us? Our God is with us, Im-man-u-

el! For all those who dwell in the shad-ow of death, a

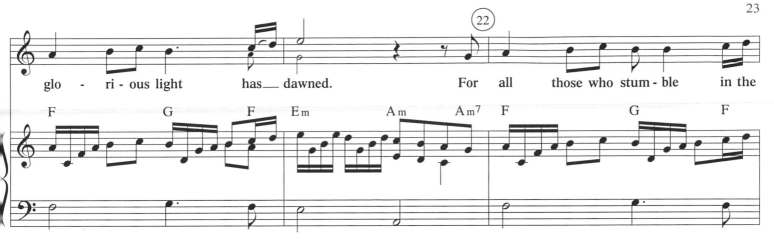

glo - ri - ous light has dawned. For all those who stum - ble in the

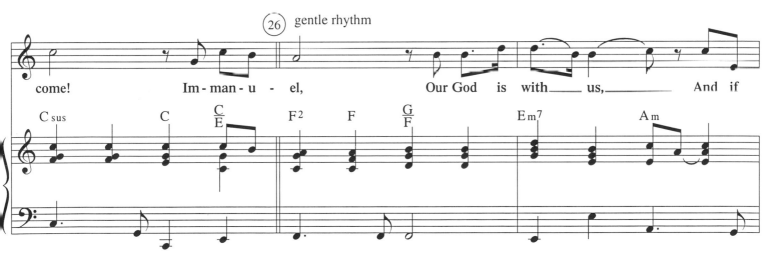

dark - ness, Be - hold! Your Light has

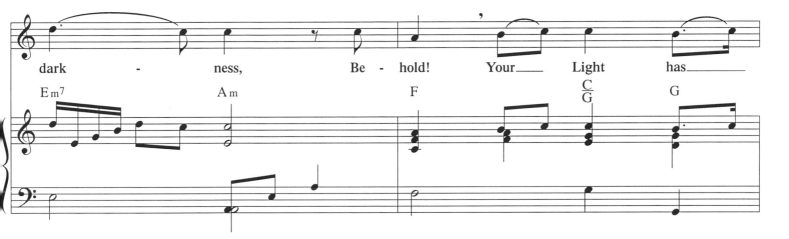

come! Im - man - u - el, Our God is with us, And if

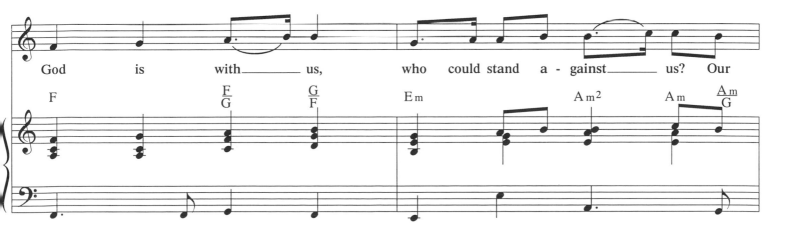

God is with us, who could stand a - gainst us? Our

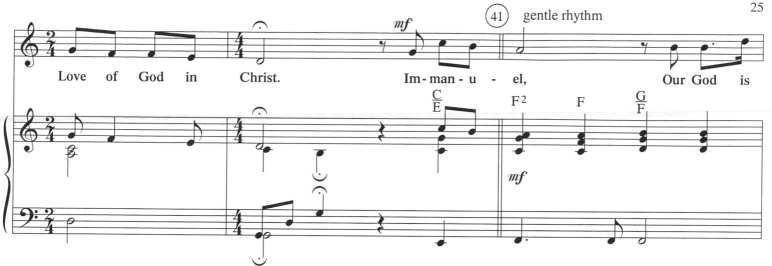

Love of God in Christ. Im-man-u-el, Our God is

with_____ us,_____ And if God is with_____ us,

who could stand a-gainst____ us? Our God is with us, Im-man-u-el! Our_

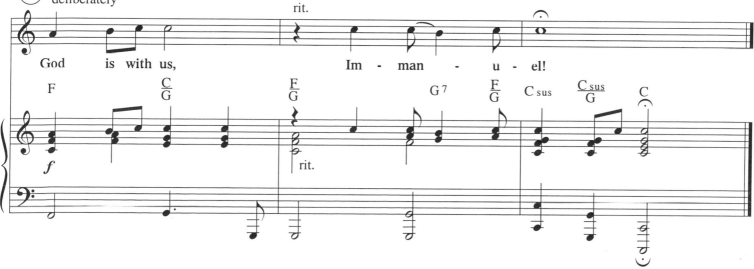

God is with us, Im-man-u-el!

That Beautiful Name

with

Take the Name of Jesus with You

JEAN PERRY

MABEL JOHNSTON CAMP
Arranged by Marty Parks

Expressively ♩ = ca. 72

mf ③ *"Take the Name of Jesus with You"*

Pre - cious name, O how sweet! Hope of earth and joy of heav'n! Pre - cious name, O how sweet! Hope of earth and joy of heav'n!

Chords:
Gm7 F2/A B♭ Dm/B C7sus C7 F F/A B♭2 B♭ B♭6

F2 F Csus/C F FM7 Dm7 Gm Gm7 C7 F F/A

B♭2 B♭ B♭m/G B♭/G E/C C13 F

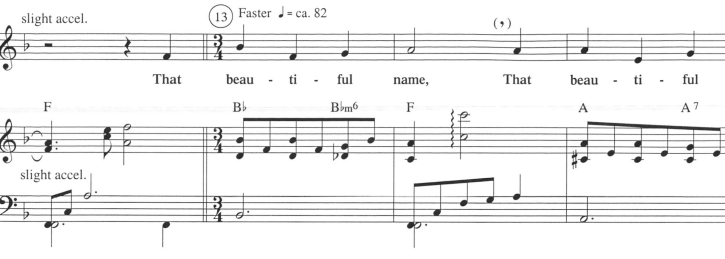

slight accel.   (13) Faster ♩= ca. 82

That beau - ti - ful name, That beau - ti - ful

slight accel.

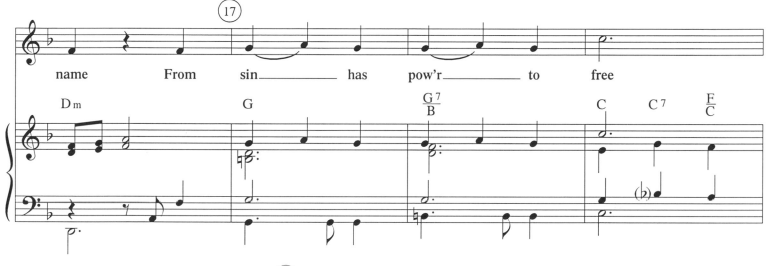

(17)

name From sin_____ has pow'r_____ to free

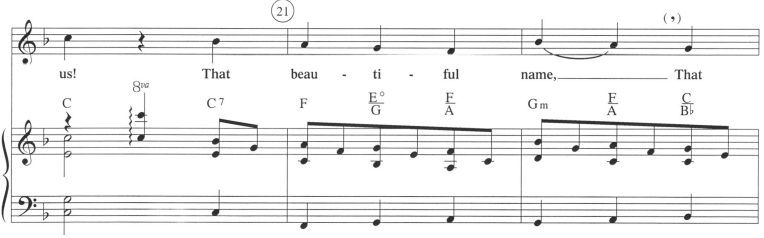

(21)

us! That beau - ti - ful name,_____ That

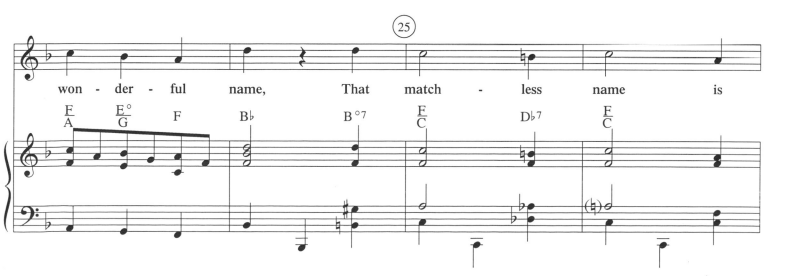

(25)

won - der - ful name, That match - less name is

Je - sus! _____ I know of a

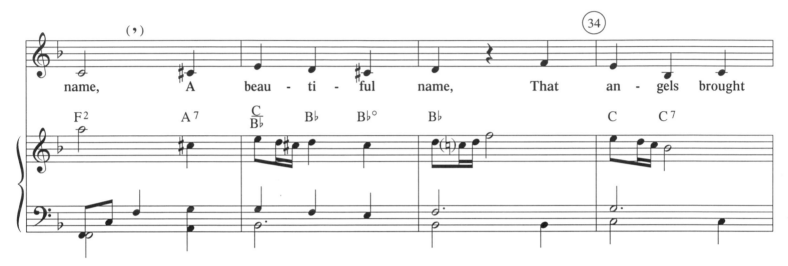

name, A beau - ti - ful name, That an - gels brought

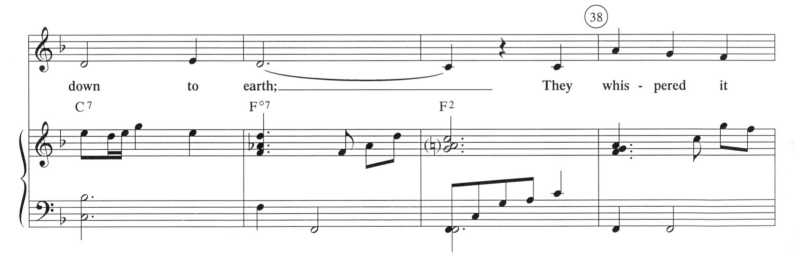

down to earth; _____ They whis - pered it

low, One night long a - go, To a maid - en of

low - ly birth. I know of a

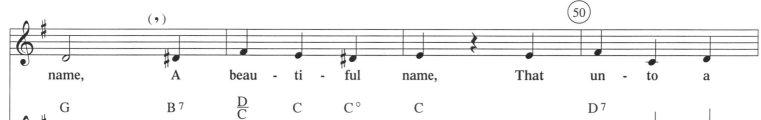

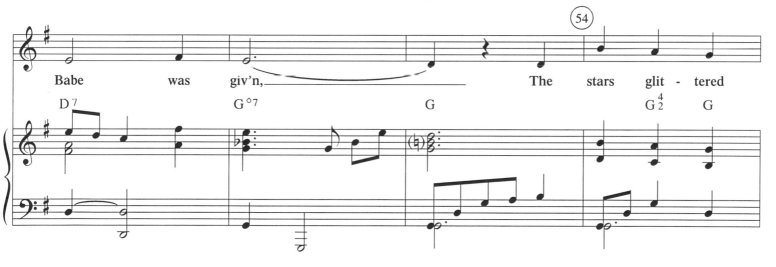

name, A beau - ti - ful name, That un - to a

Babe was giv'n,_____ The stars glit - tered

bright through - out that glad night, And an - gels praised

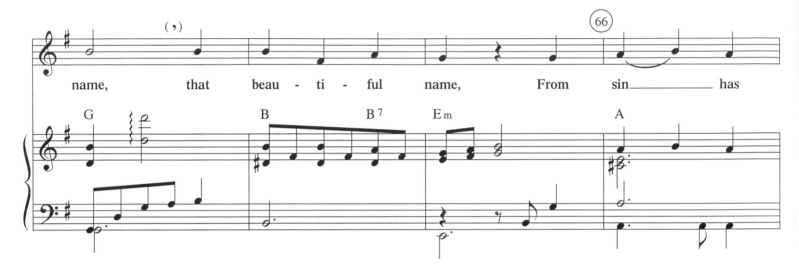

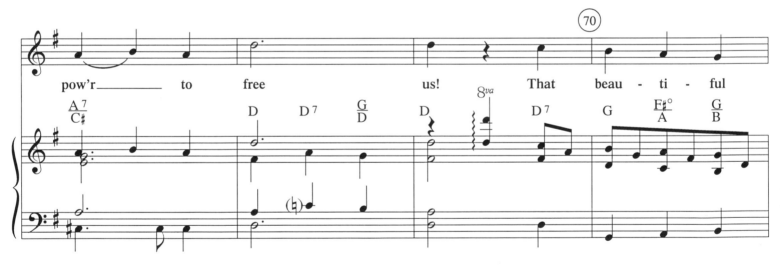

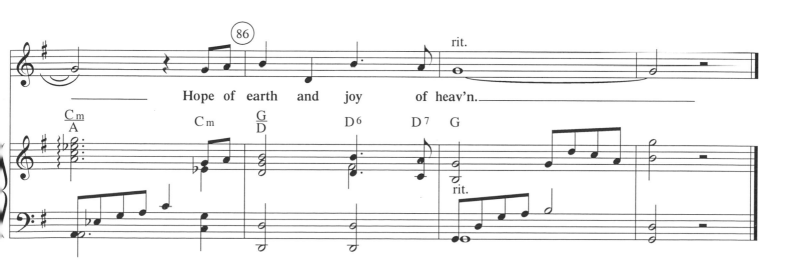

Redeeming Love

GLORIA GAITHER

WILLIAM J. GAITHER
Arranged by Marty Parks

love that knows no lim - it; Re - deem - ing

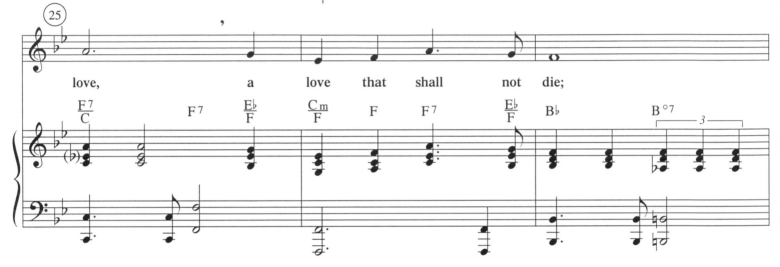

love, a love that shall not die;

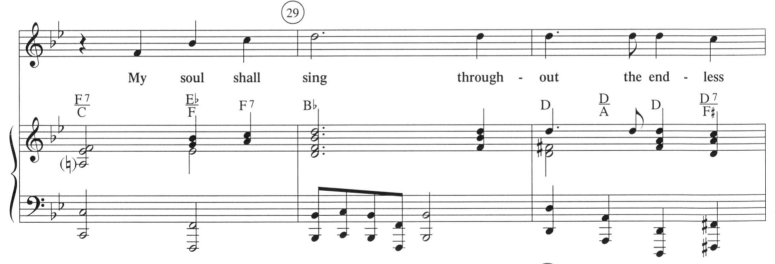

My soul shall sing through - out the end - less

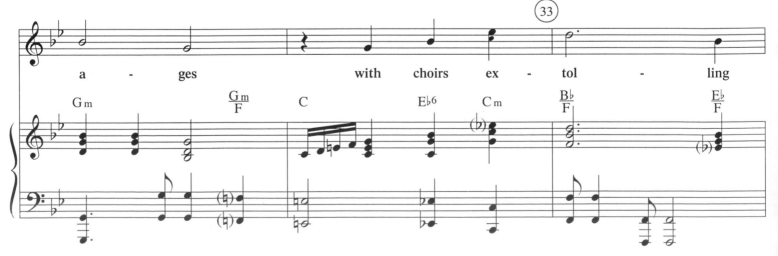

a - ges with choirs ex - tol - ling

This World

Words and Music by
OREN PARIS
Arranged by Marty Parks

Smooth and steady ♩ = ca.122

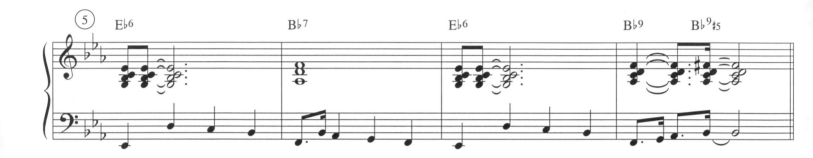

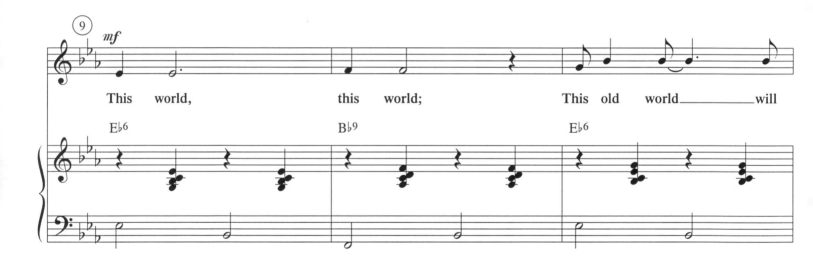

This world, this world; This old world_____will

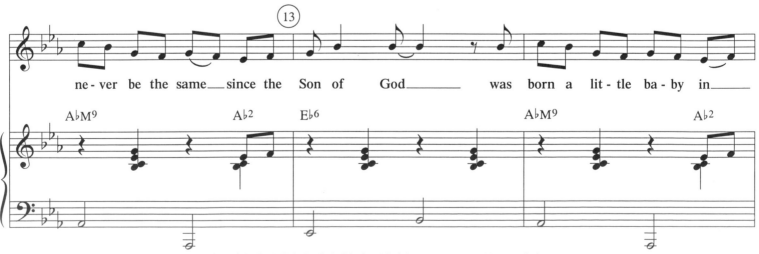

ne - ver be the same___since the Son of God_____ was born a lit - tle ba - by in

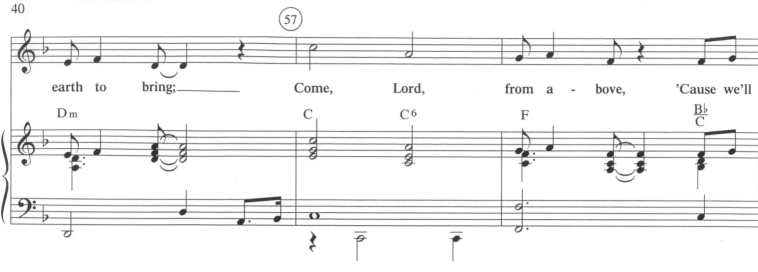

earth to bring;_____ Come, Lord, from a - bove, 'Cause we'll

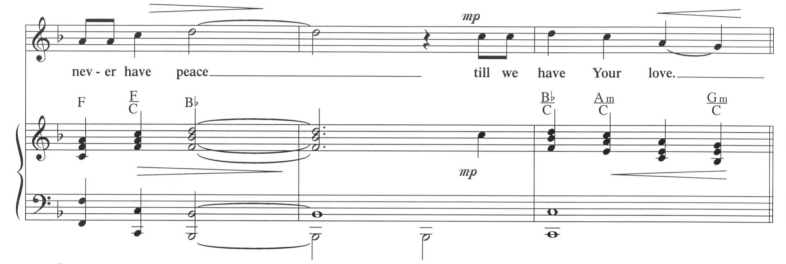

nev - er have peace_____ till we have Your love._____

This world, this world; This old world_____ will

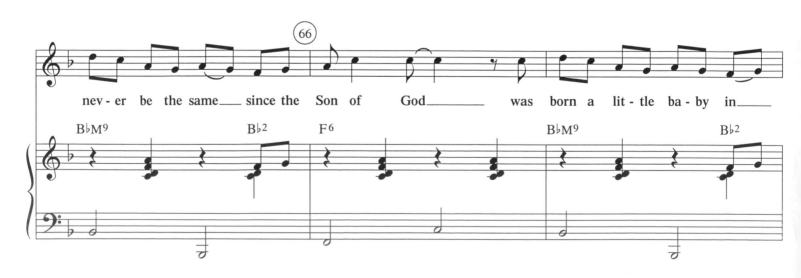

nev - er be the same___ since the Son of God_____ was born a lit - tle ba - by in

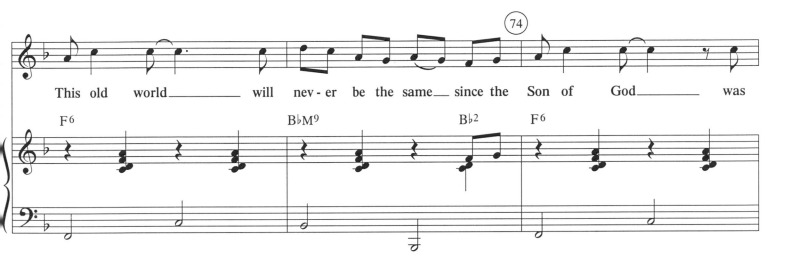

I Will Sing Of My Redeemer

PHILIP P. BLISS

JAMES McGRANAHAN
Arranged by Marty Parks

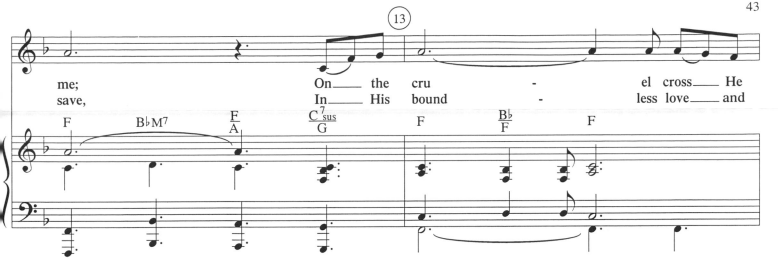

(to pg. 42, meas. 9)

The Love of God

FREDERICK M. LEHMAN,
MEIR BEN ISAAC NEHORAI,
and KEN BIBLE

FREDERICK M. LEHMAN
Arranged by Marty Parks

*Verse 1 by Frederick M. Lehman,; verse 2 by Meir Ben Isaac Nehorai; verse 3 by Ken Bible

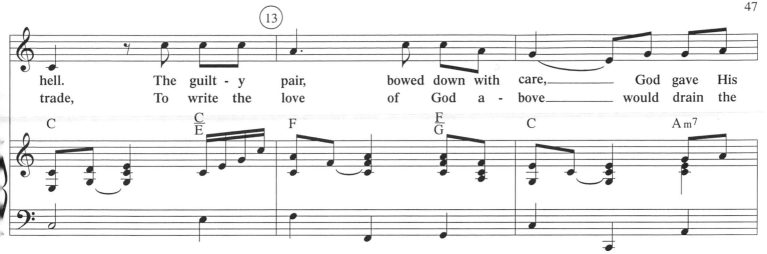

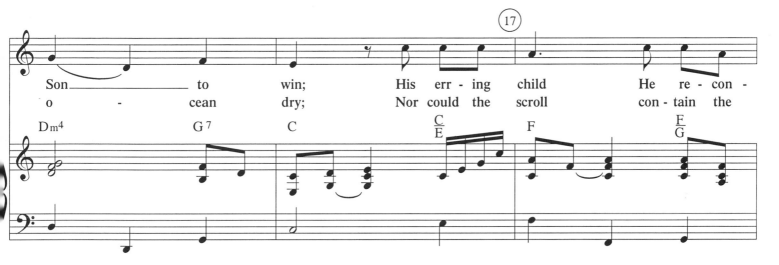

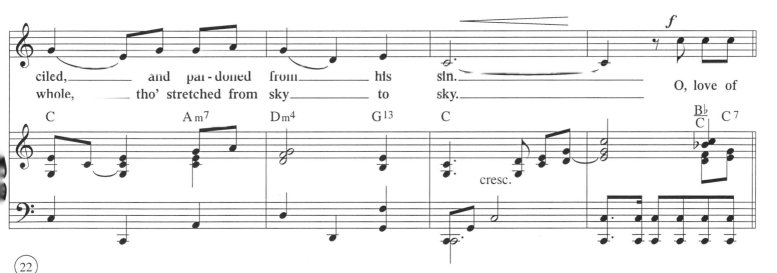

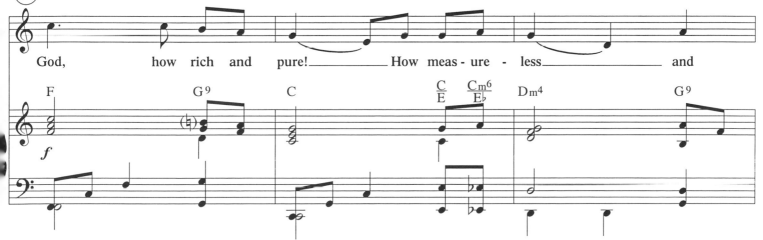

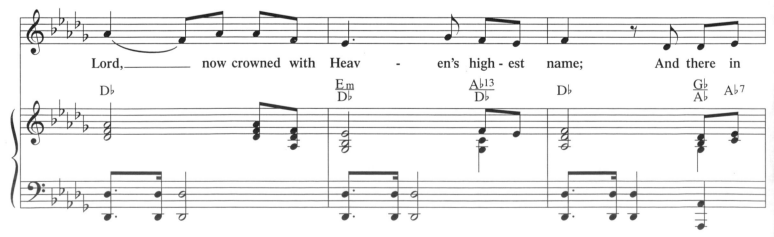

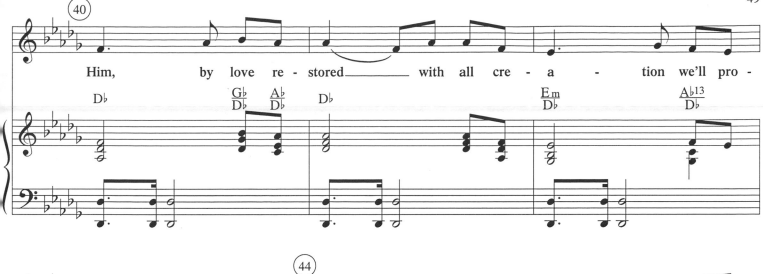

Him, by love re-stored _____ with all cre-a - tion we'll pro-

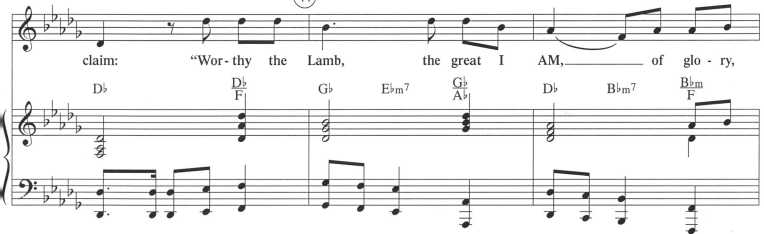

claim: "Wor-thy the Lamb, the great I AM, _____ of glo-ry,

pow'r _____ and might!" With joy we'll trace His bound-less

grace _____ in all it's depth _____ and height. _____ O love of

Alleluia! Alleluia! Give Thanks
to the Risen Lord

Words and Music by
DONALD FISHEL
Arranged by Marty Parks

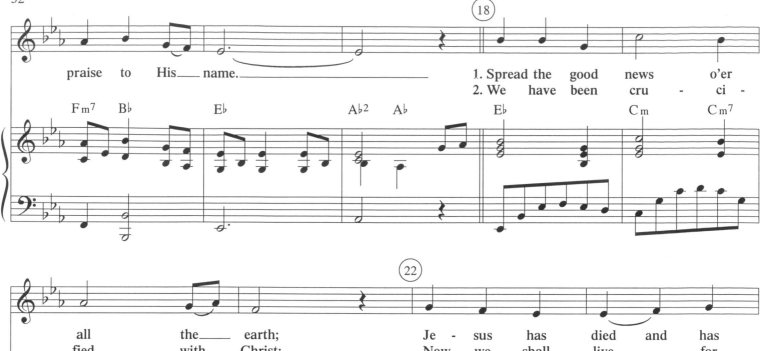

praise to His name. 1. Spread the good news o'er
2. We have been cru - ci -

Fm⁷ B♭ E♭ A♭2 A♭ E♭ Cm Cm⁷

all the earth; Je - sus has died and has
fied with Christ; Now we shall live for -

Fm⁷ B♭sus B♭7 E♭ Fm/E♭ E♭ Cm Fm/C Cm⁷

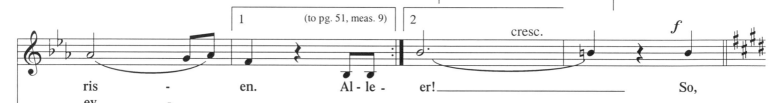

(to pg. 51, meas. 9)

1. 2. cresc. *f*

ris - en. Al - le - er! So,
ev -

Fm⁷ B♭sus B♭7 B♭sus B♭ Bsus B

cresc.

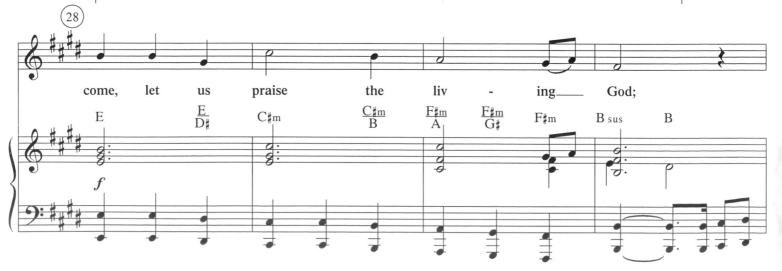

come, let us praise the liv - ing God;

E E/D♯ C♯m C♯m/B F♯m/A F♯m/G♯ F♯m Bsus B

f

Joy - ful - ly sing to our Sav - ior!_____

rit.   Broader tempo

Al - le - lu - ia, Al - le - lu - ia! Give___ thanks to the

ris - en Lord; Al - le - lu - ia, Al - le - lu - ia! Give___ praise to His

name!   Al - le - lu - ia!

I Know That My Redeemer Lives

SAMUEL MEDLEY

JOHN HATTON
Arranged by Marty Parks

He lives, He lives____ who____ once____ was____ dead;

He lives, my Ev - - er - last - ing Head!

He lives to bless me____ with His____

love; He lives to plead for me a -

bove. He lives my hun - gry_____ soul_____ to_____

feed; He lives to help in time____ of need.

He lives, and grants me_____ dai - ly_____

breath; He lives, and I shall con - quer

Our God Reigns

Words and Music by
LEONARD E. SMITH, JR.
Arranged by Marty Parks

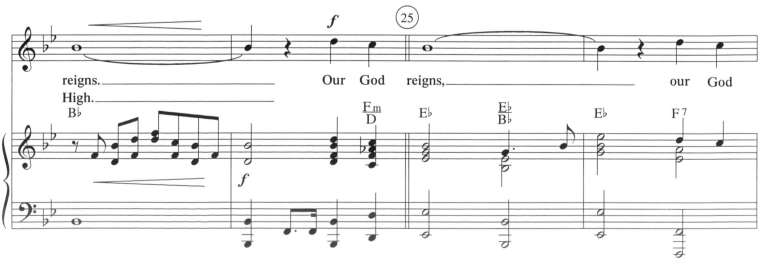

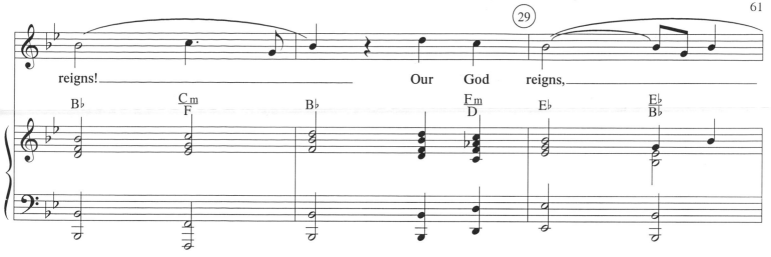

reigns!_____ Our God reigns,_____

_____ our God reigns. 2. He had no

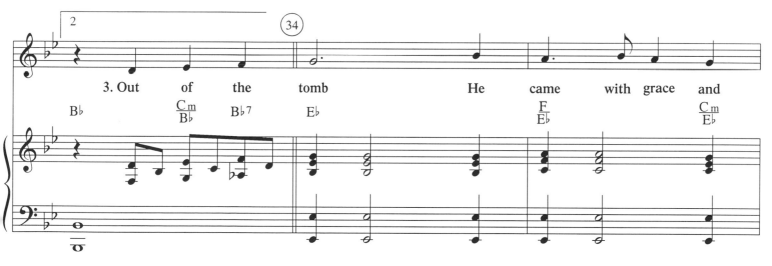

3. Out of the tomb He came with grace and

maj - es - ty, He is a - live,

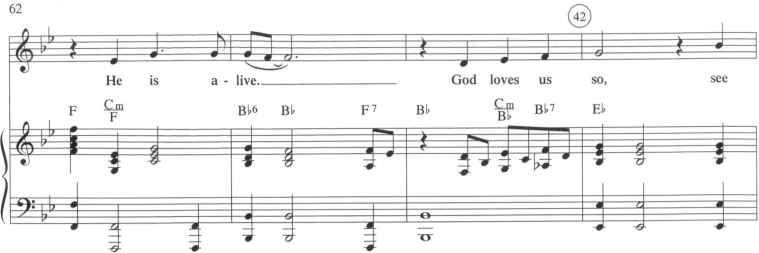

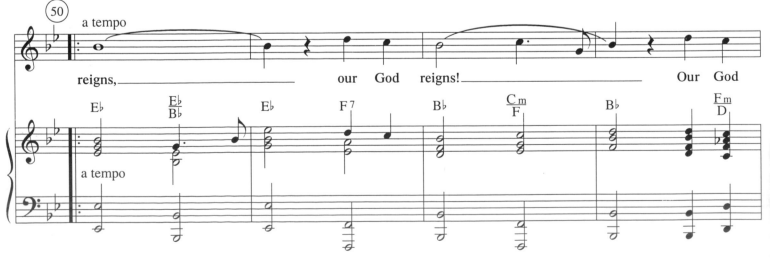

Arise, My Love

Words and Music by
EDDIE CARSWELL
Arranged by Marty Parks

Not a word was heard   at the tomb that day,

Just shuf - fling sol - diers' feet   as they guard - ed the grave;

The earth trem - bled and the tomb be - gan to shake,

Like light - ning from heav - en the stone rolled a - way;

And as dead men, the guards stood there in fright, As the

pow - er of love____ dis - played its might.____ "A - rise,

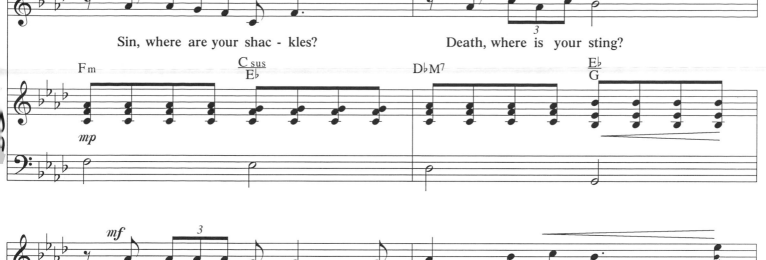

Sin, where are your shac - kles?　　Death, where is your sting?

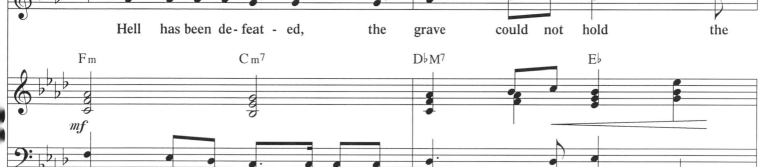

Hell　has been de - feat - ed,　　the　grave　could not hold　　the

King!　　　　　　　　　　　"A - rise, rise!　　　A -

D.S. al Coda ⊕ CODA
(to pg. 68, meas.43)

rise!"

Hallelujah! What a Savior!

PHILIP P. BLISS

MARTY PARKS
Arranged by Marty Parks

Grace

with
Grace Greater than Our Sin

Words and Music by
PAMELA FURR, WAYNE HAUN
and RAYMOND C. DAVIS
Arranged by Marty Parks

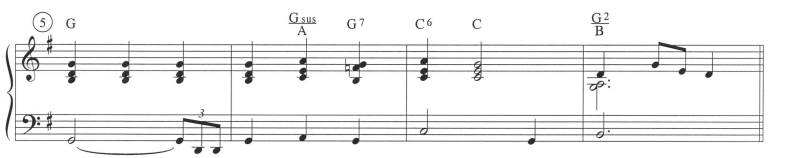

Tears of frus-tra-tion_____ as love passed me by,

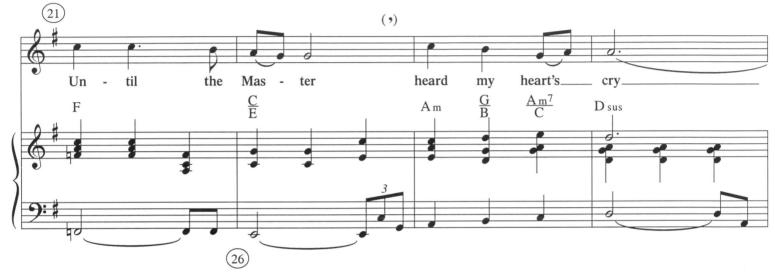

Un-til the Mas-ter heard my heart's__ cry_____

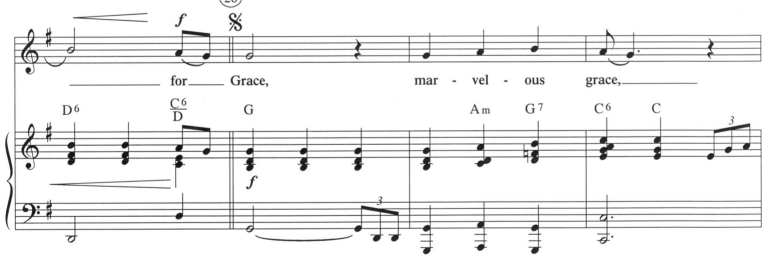

_____ for ___ Grace, mar-vel-ous grace,_____

I need-ed grace to par-don and make me

Pray - ing for mer - cy with no - where to hide;

There was a so - lace search - ing for me, And

grace o - ver - flow - ing set my soul free!

D.S. al Coda ⊕ CODA
(to pg. 74, meas. 26)

It was grace.

Driving!

*"Grace Greater than Our Sin"

Love Is Why

W.F. LAKEY and
VEP ELLIS

DAVID ELLIS and VEP ELLIS
Arranged by Marty Parks

1. He nev-er said I'd have sil-ver or gold, Yet He has prom - ised me
2. I was a-stray, full of sin with it's shame, There was no peace with - in,

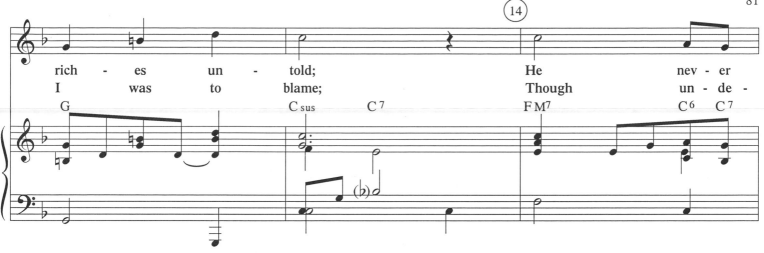

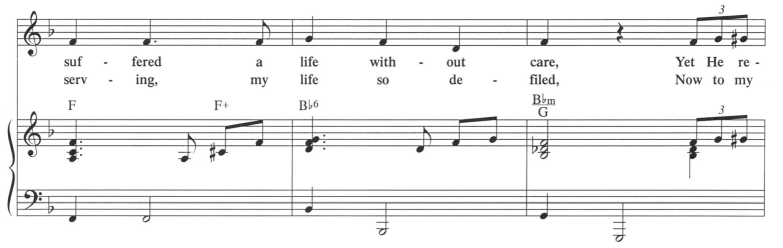

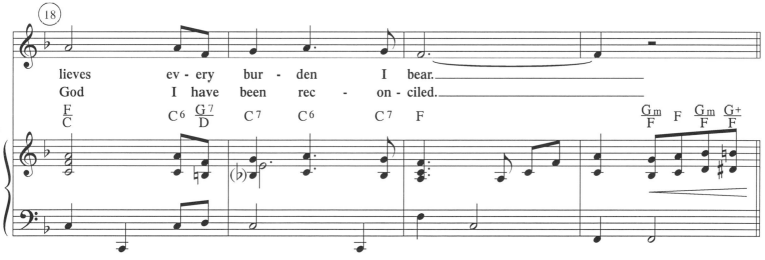

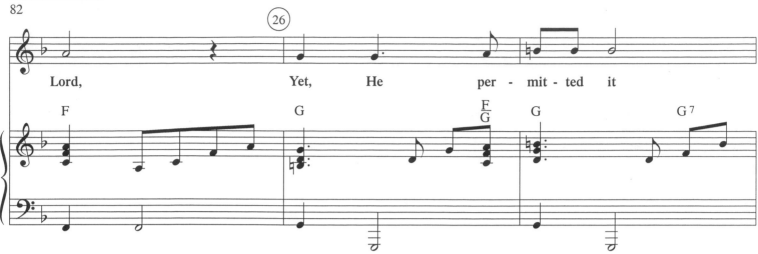

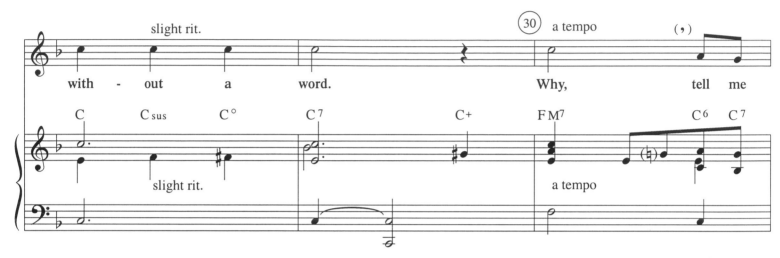

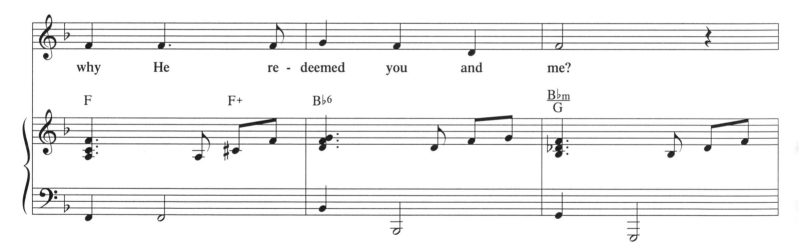

Hallelujah to the Lamb

Words and Music by
CONRAD COOK
Arranged by Marty Parks

Gospel Feel ♩ = ca. 78

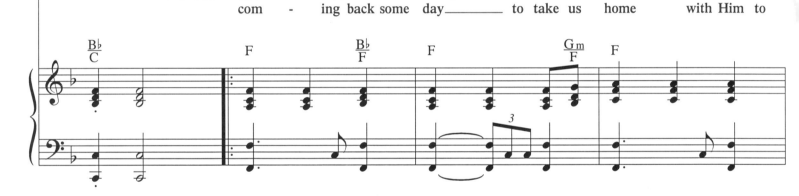

1. It was told that He would come, and the race He would
com - ing back some day to take us home with Him to

run, It would end on an old rug - ged cross;
stay, Where His glo - ry for - ev - er we will share;

slain up - on a tree!_____ By His

stripes we are healed, And by His blood we are sealed! Hal - le -

lu - jah to the Lamb_____ of God!_____

(to pg. 84, meas. 5)

2. Church, He's

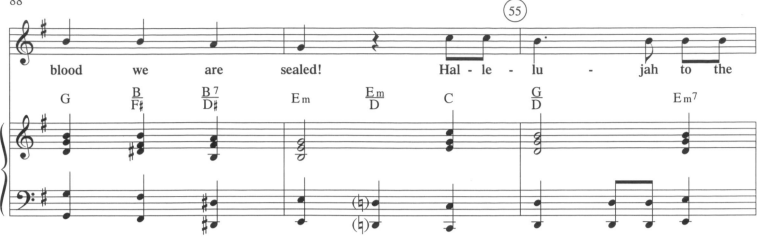

blood we are sealed! Hal - le - lu - jah to the

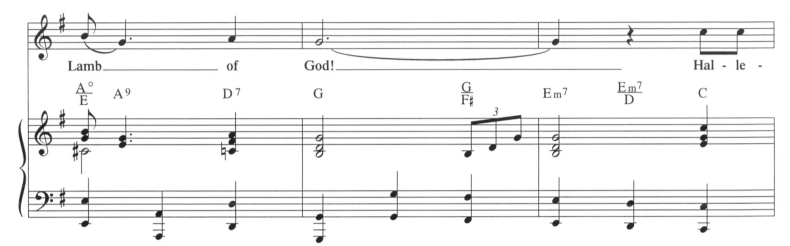

Lamb_____ of God!_____ Hal - le -

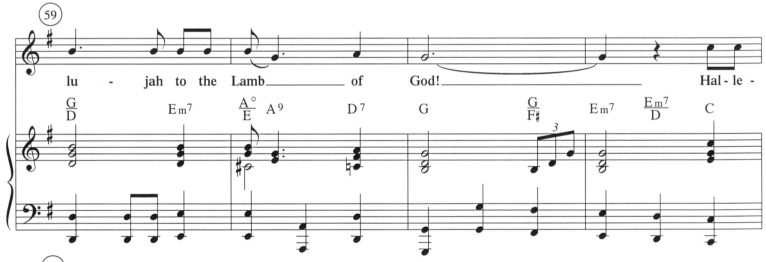

lu - jah to the Lamb_____ of God!_____ Hal - le -

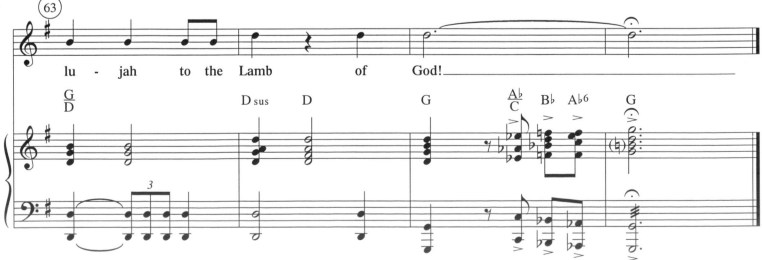

lu - jah to the Lamb of God!_____

I Pledge Allegiance to the Lamb

Words and Music by
RAY BOLTZ
Arranged by Marty Parks

1. I have heard how Chris-tians
(2. Now the) years have come, the

long a - go were brought be - fore a ty - rant's throne; They were
years have gone; The cause of Je - sus still goes on. Now our

Statue of Liberty

Words and Music by
NEIL ENLOE
Arranged by Marty Parks

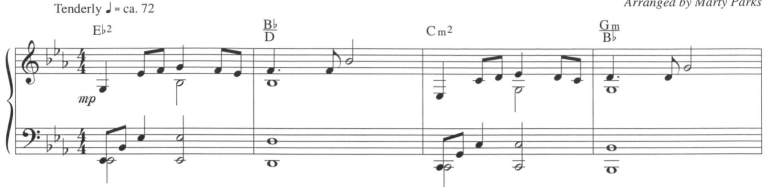

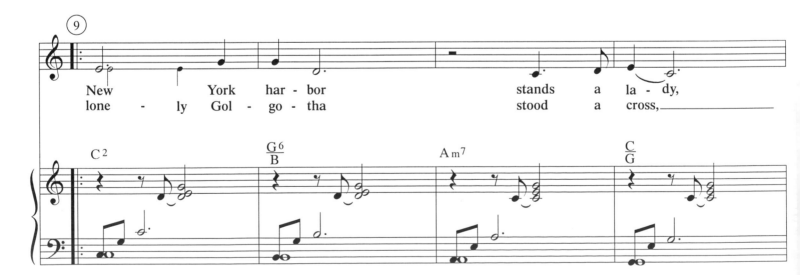

New York har-bor stands a la-dy,

lone - ly Gol - go - tha stood a cross,

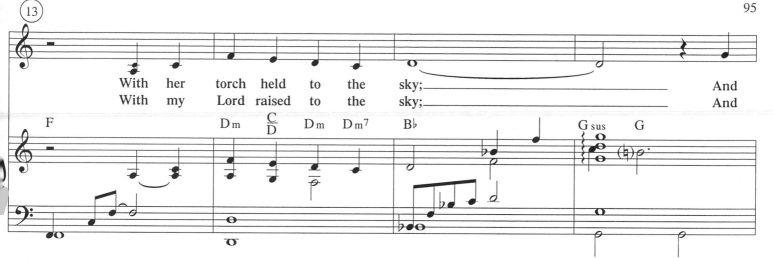

13

With her torch held to the sky;_____ And
With my Lord raised to the sky;_____ And

17

all who see_____ her know she
all who kneel_____ there live for-

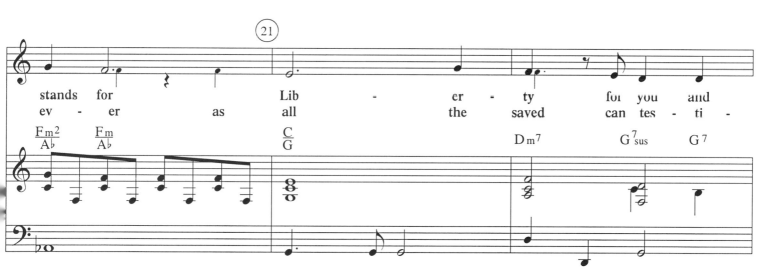

21

stands for as Lib - er - ty for you and
ev - er as all the saved can tes - ti -

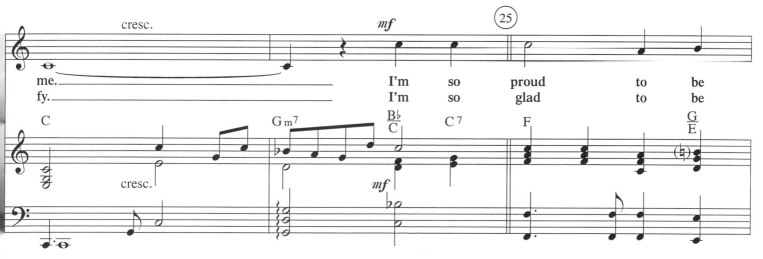

25

me._____ I'm so proud to be
fy._____ I'm so glad to be

It's Time to Pray

Words and Music by
JOHN W. PETERSON
Arranged by Marty Parks

o'er us,   It's time to seek   His

help with - out de - lay; The world is

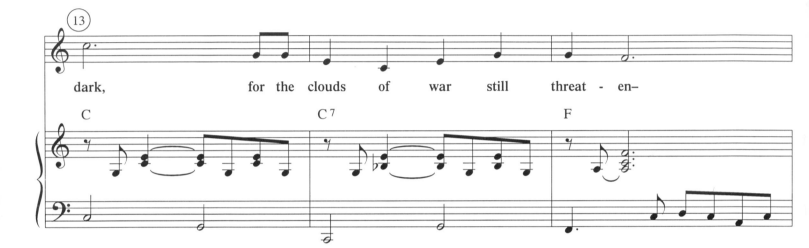

dark, for the clouds of war still threat - en–

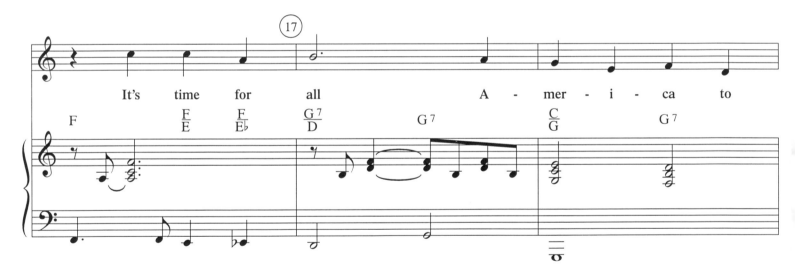

It's time for all A - mer - i - ca to

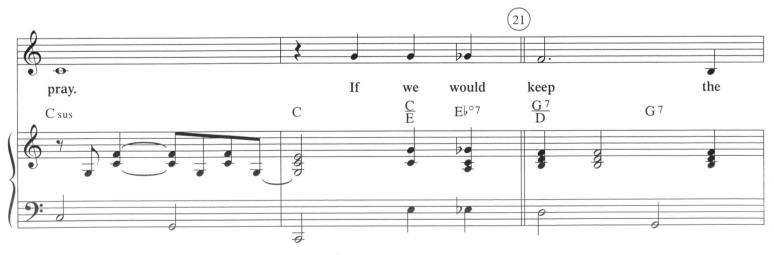

pray. If we would keep the

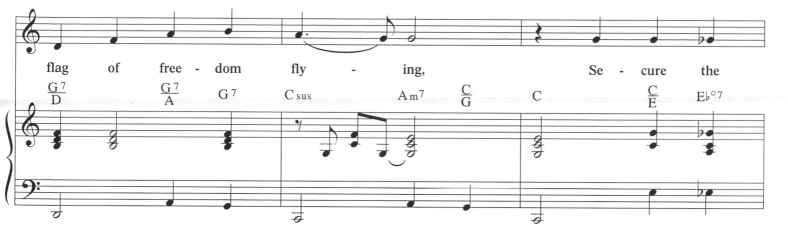

flag of free - dom fly - ing, Se - cure the

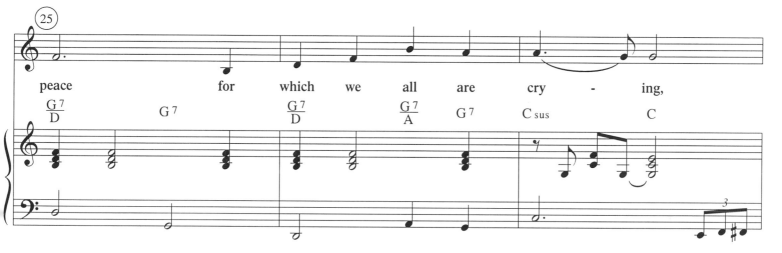

peace for which we all are cry - ing,

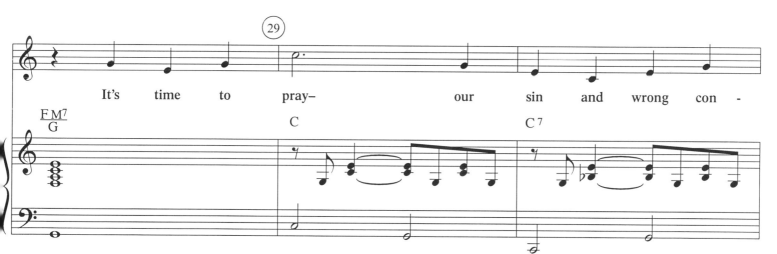

It's time to pray– our sin and wrong con -

2nd time to Coda ⊕ ③③
(to pg. 103, meas. 45)

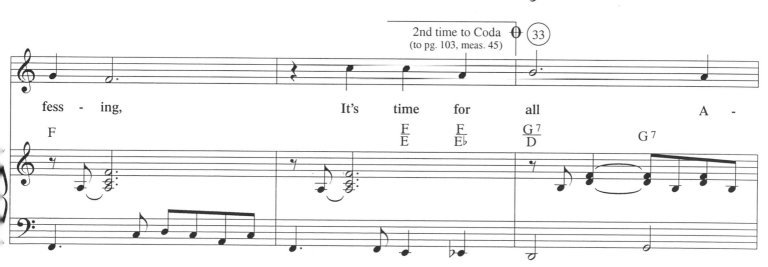

fess - ing, It's time for all A -

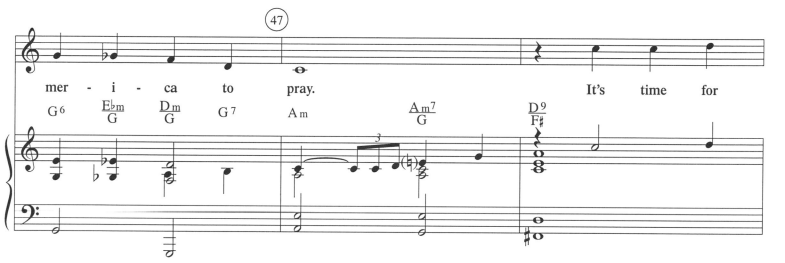

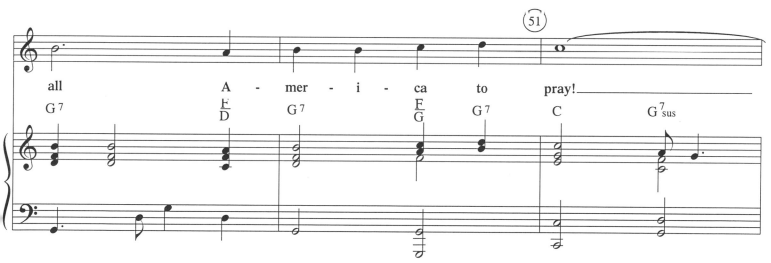

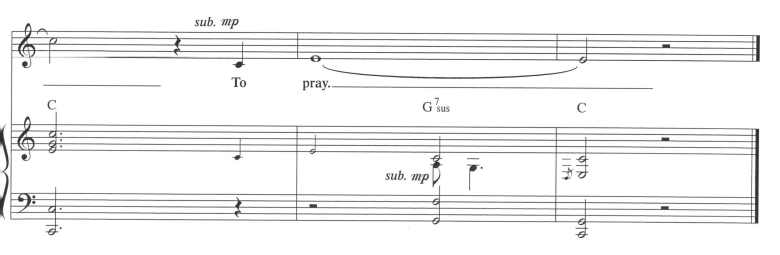

Keep Freedom's Dream Alive

DEBRA GRUBBS and MARTY PARKS

MARTY PARKS
Arranged by Marty Parks

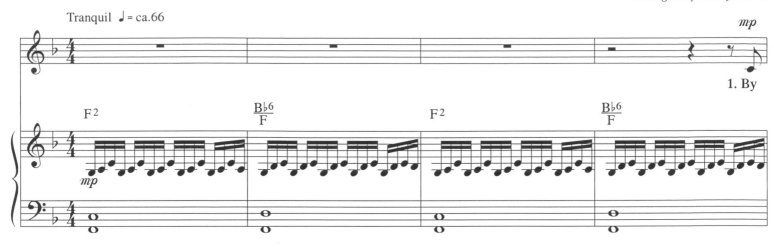

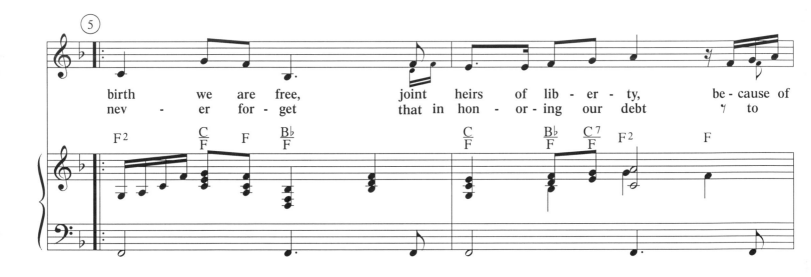

Jesus, We Just Want to Thank You

with
We Are So Blessed

GLORIA GAITHER
and WILLIAM J. GAITHER

WILLIAM J. GAITHER
Arranged by Marty Parks

Lightly ♩ = ca. 64

Je - sus, we just want to thank You,_____ Je - sus, we just want to

can't un - der - stand_____ why You've loved us so
words that can say,_____ _____ "Thank You

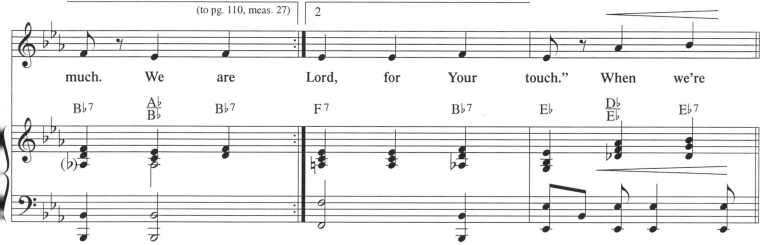

much. We are Lord, for Your touch." When we're

emp - ty_____ You fill us_____ 'til we o - ver - flow; When we're

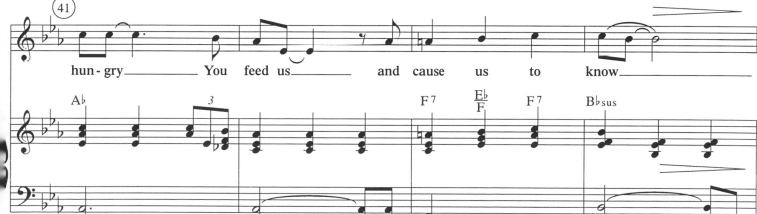

hun - gry_____ You feed us_____ and cause us to know_____

(to pg. 110, meas. 27)

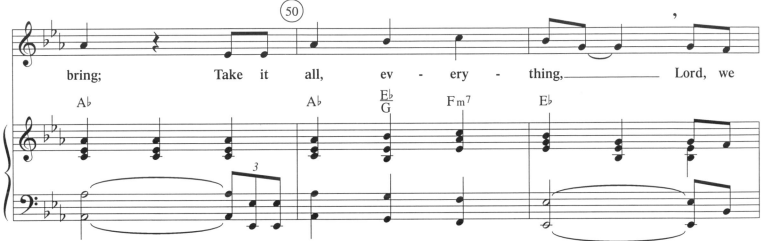

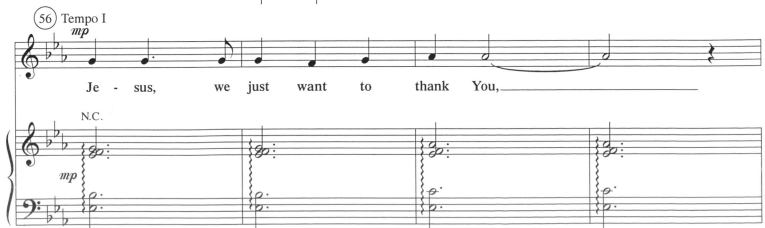

Give Thanks

Words and Music by
HENRY SMITH
Arranged by Marty Parks

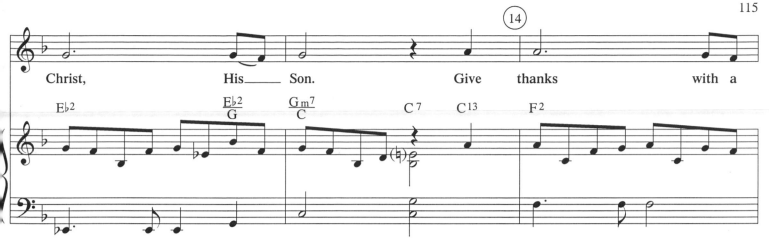

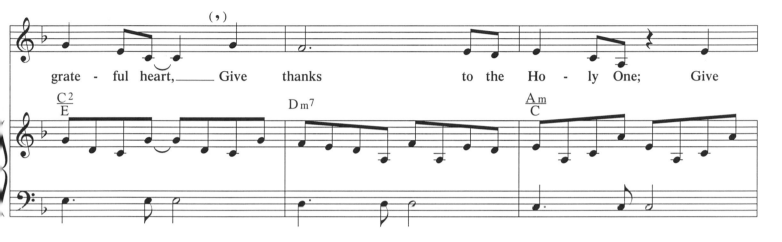

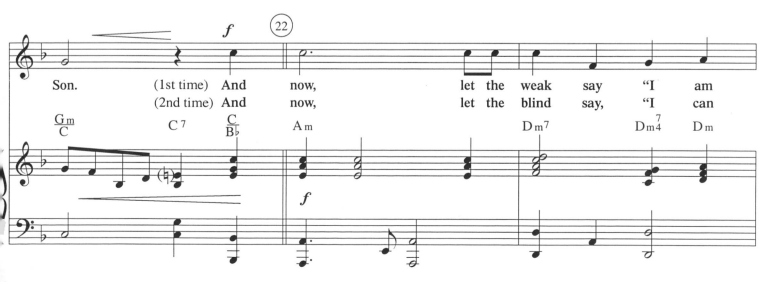

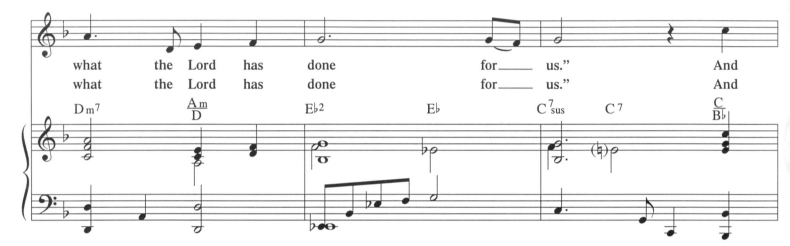

All the Glory Belongs to Jesus

GLORIA GAITHER

WILLIAM J. GAITHER
Arranged by Marty Parks

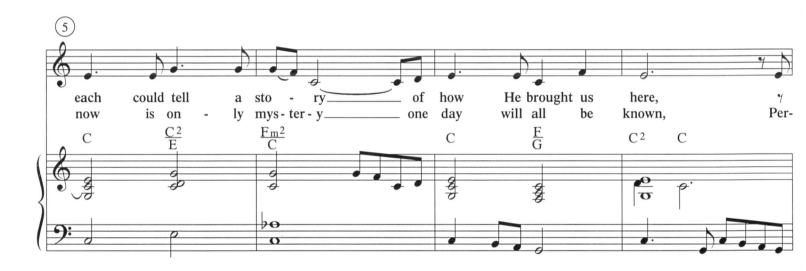

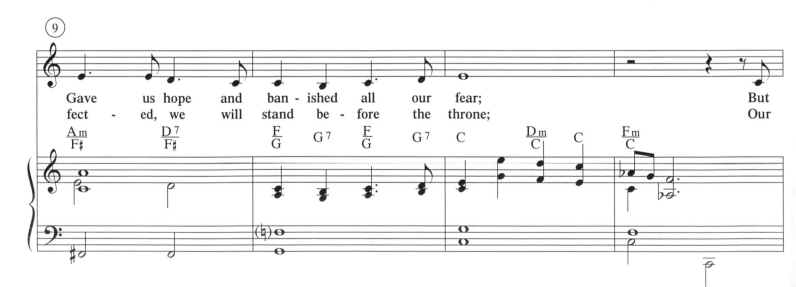

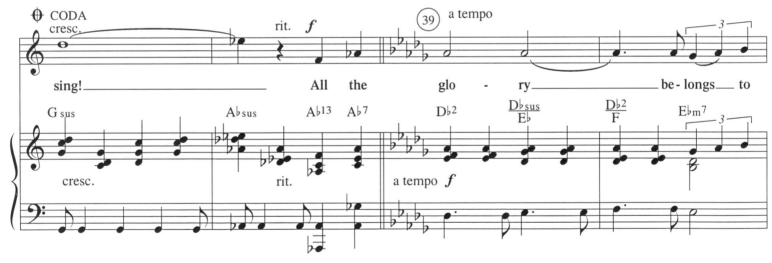

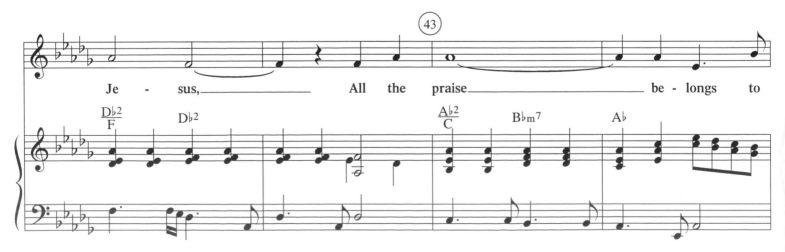

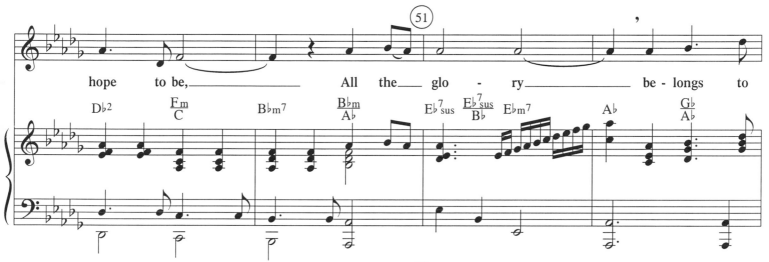

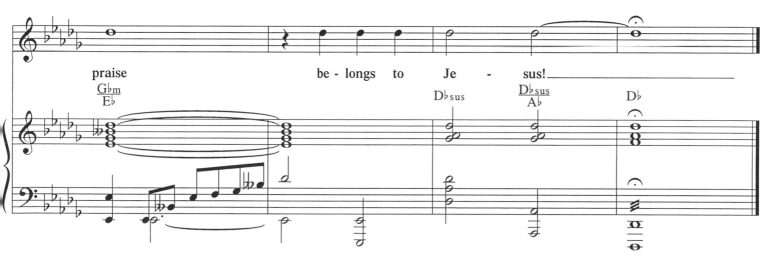

I'm Forever Grateful

Words and Music by
MARK ALTROGGE
Arranged by Marty Parks

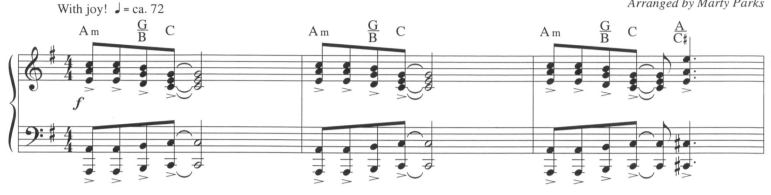

And I'm for-ev-er grate-ful to You,___

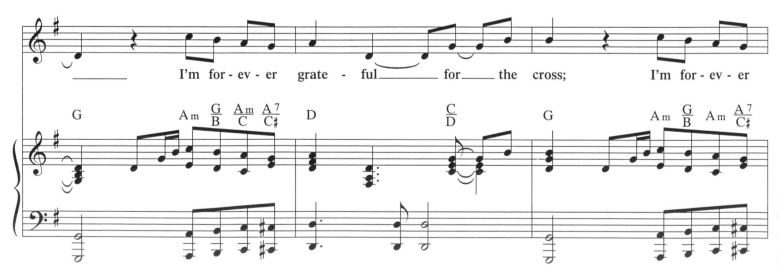

___ I'm for-ev-er grate-ful___ for___ the cross; I'm for-ev-er

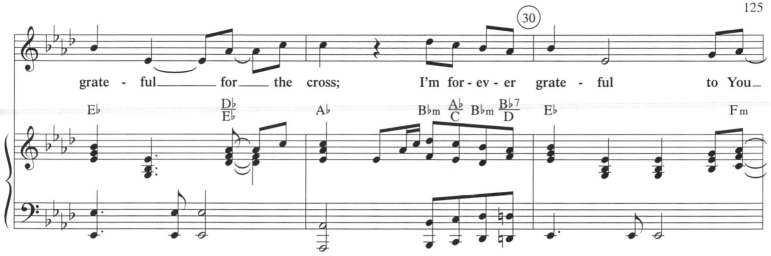

grate - ful____ for ____ the cross; I'm for - ev - er grate - ful to You____

_____ that____ You came_____ to seek and save_____ the lost.____

_____ To seek and save_____ the lost._____ And I'm for - ev - er

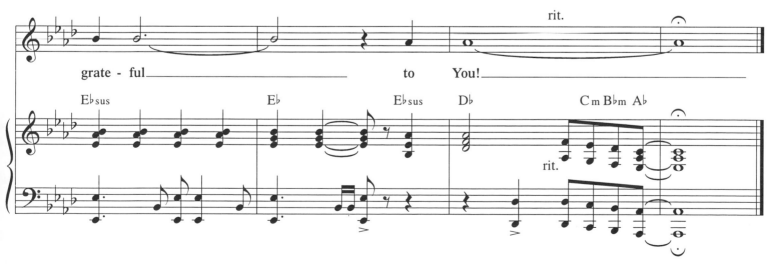

grate - ful_____ to You!_____

We Praise Thee, O God, Our Redeemer

JULIA C. CORY

Netherlands Folk Song
Arranged by Marty Parks

Brightly ♩ = ca. 102

1. We praise Thee, O God, our Re-deem-er, Cre-
3. With voic-es u-nit-ed our prais-es we

a-tor; In grate-ful de-vo-tion our trib-ute we bring. We
of-fer, And glad-ly our songs of true wor-ship we raise. Thy

guide Thou hast been. When per - ils o'er - take us, Thou

wilt___ not for - sake us, And with Thy help, O Lord,___ life's

rit.

D.C. al Coda ⊕ CODA
(to pg. 126, meas. 1)

bat - tles we win.   praise.   A - men!

rit.

f

A - men!___

The Blessing Song

Words and Music by
NANCY GORDON, LINDA WALKER
and JAMIE HARVILL
Arranged by Marty Parks

May your fu-ture be a ho-ly leg-a-cy; May
May your fu-ture be a ho-ly leg-a-cy; May

bless-ings be up-on you pre-cious ba-by.
bless-ings be up-on your chil-dren's chil-dren.

1 (to pg. 129, meas. 5)
2. May

2

mf

May God bless you in your com-ing, may He

bless you in your go-ing, May your heart be ev-er know-ing the

bless - ings of the Lord. May bless - ings be up - on you, pre - cious

ba - by. May fav - or rest up - on your fam - i -

ly. May your fu - ture be a ho - ly leg - a - cy; May

bless - ings be up - on you pre - cious ba - by.

Love Gives Birth to Life

KEN BIBLE

MARTY PARKS
Arranged by Marty Parks

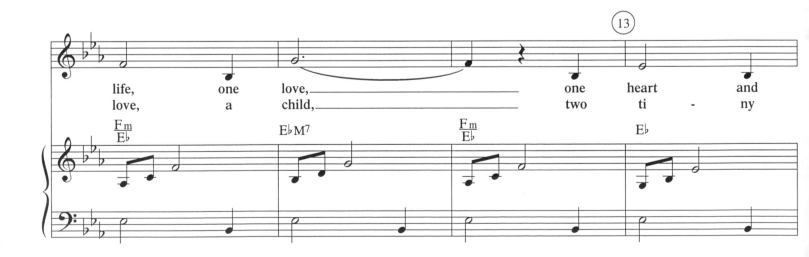

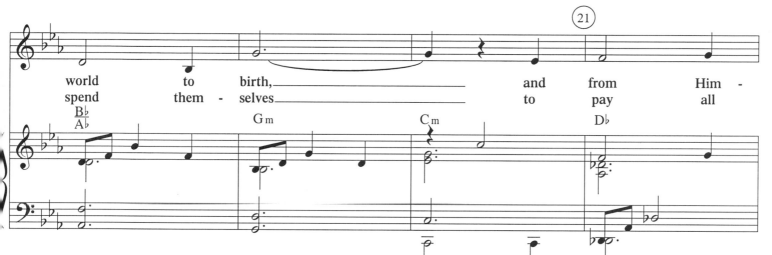
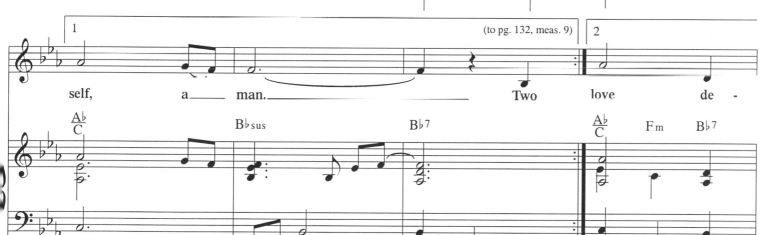
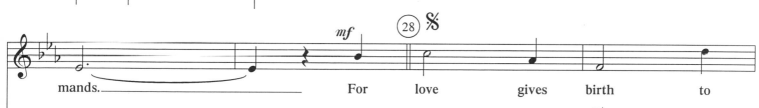
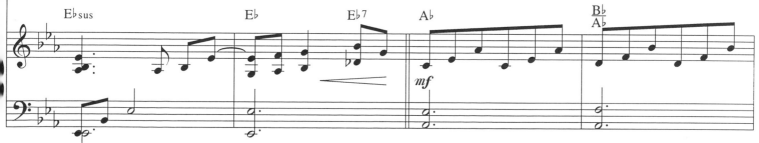

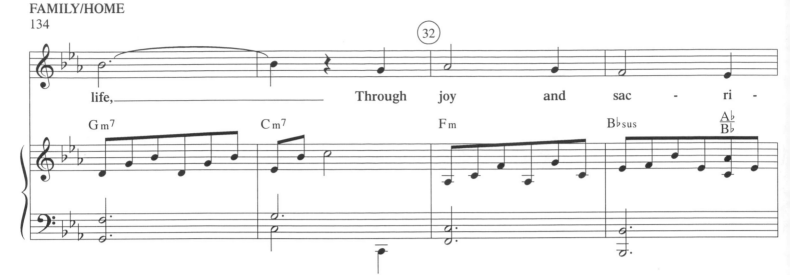

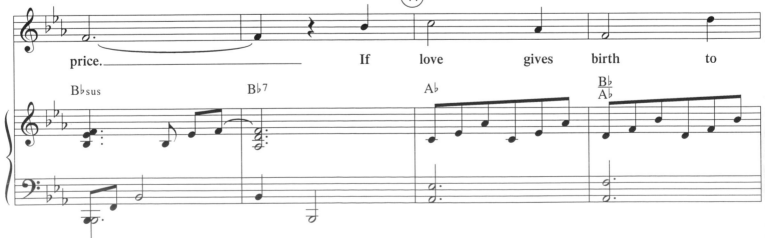

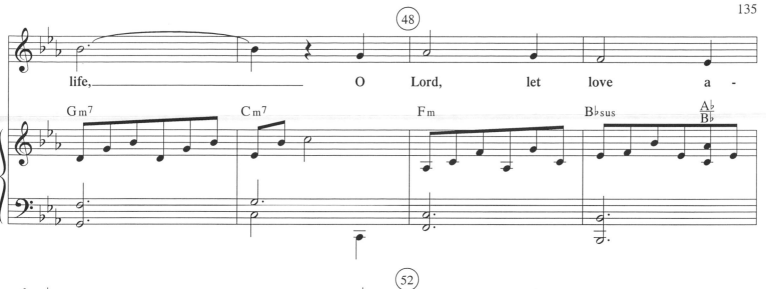

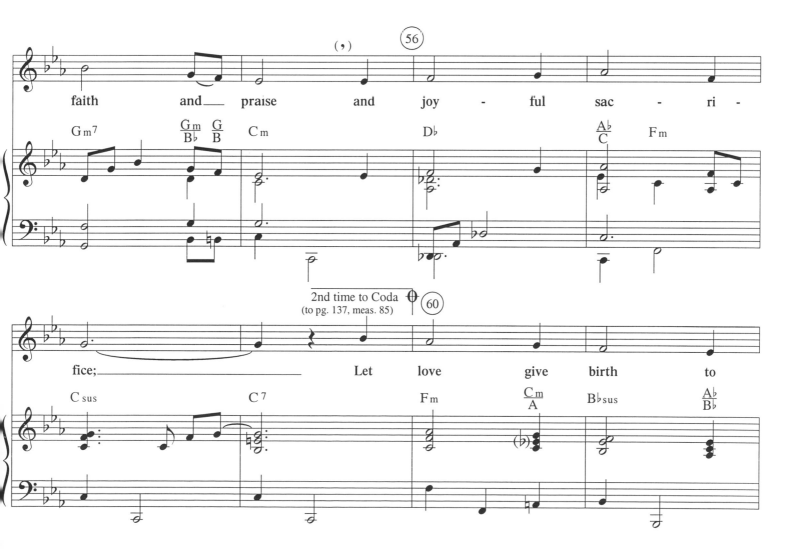

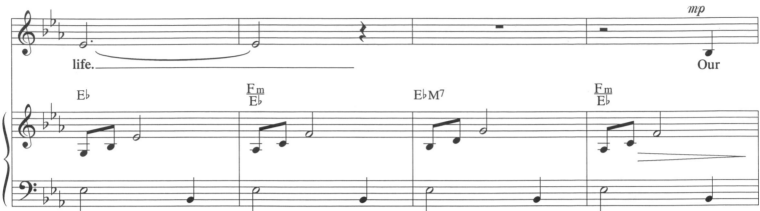

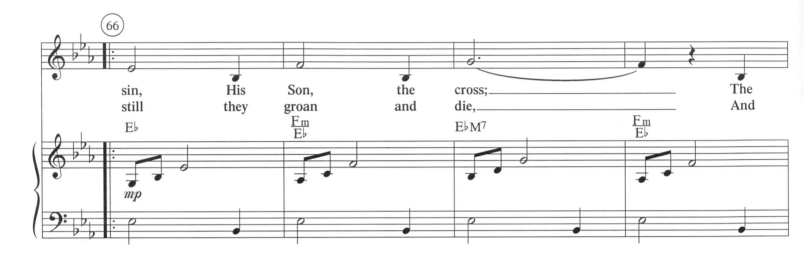

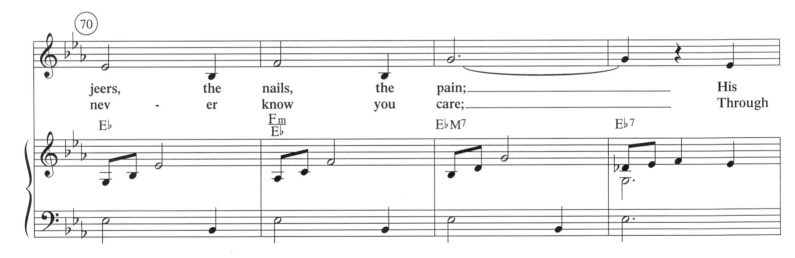

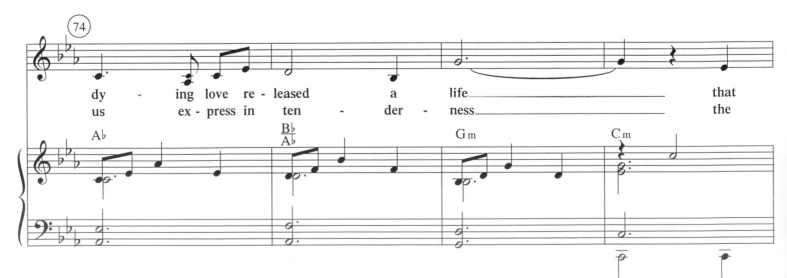

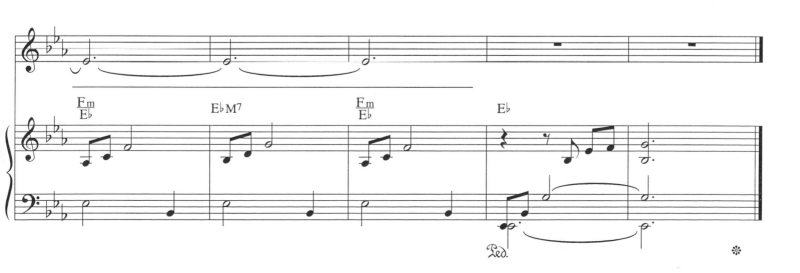

He Loves Me

Words and Music by
KEN BIBLE
Arranged by Marty Parks

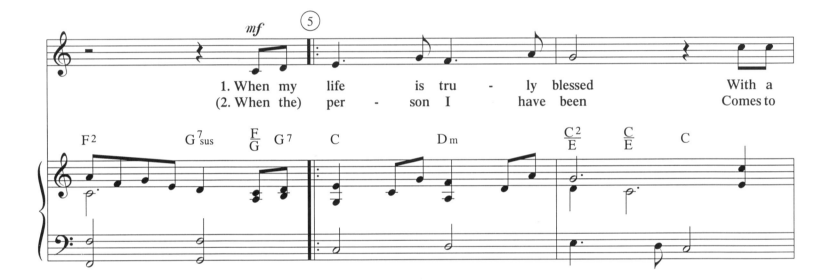

1. When my life is tru-ly blessed
(2. When the) per-son I have been

With a
Comes to

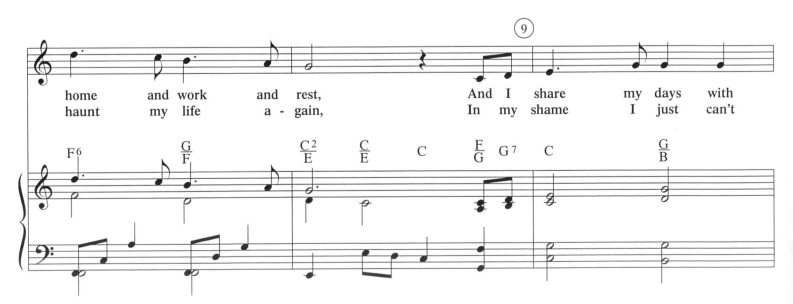

home and work and rest,
haunt my life a-gain,

And I share my days with
In my shame I just can't

My Fa - ther loves me; Each mo - ment

loves me,_____ I am His child.

He's al - ways with me, His best He

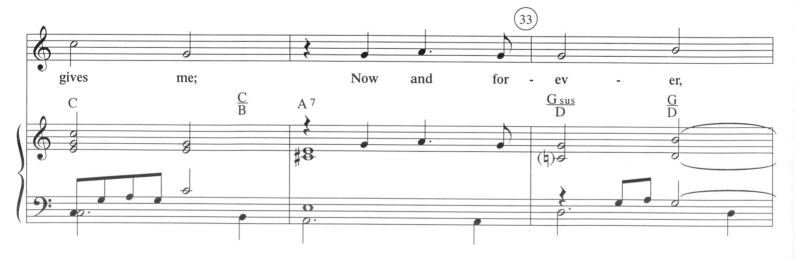

gives me; Now and for - ev - er,

The Gift of Love

HAL HOPSON
Parapharase of I Corinthians 13

HAL HOPSON
Based on a Traditional English Melody
Arranged by Marty Parks

Go There With You

Words and Music by
STEVEN CURTIS CHAPMAN
Arranged by Marty Parks

Softly intense ♩ = ca. 82

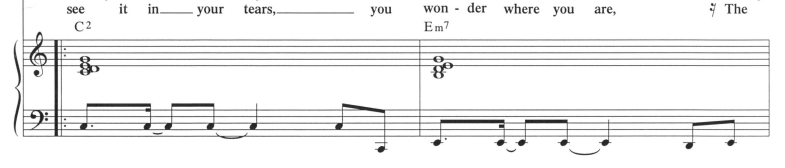

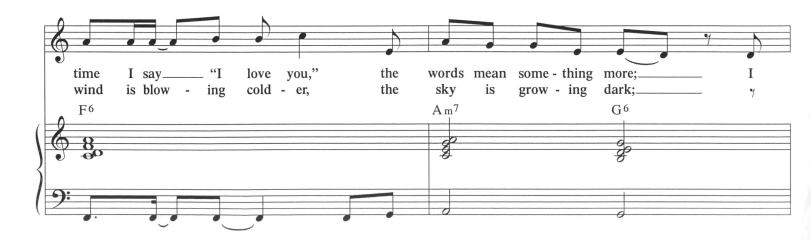

know you've heard__ me say_____ these words be - fore,_____ But ev - ery
see it in__ your tears,_____ you won - der where you are,

time I say_____ "I love you," the words mean some - thing more;_____ I
wind is blow - ing cold - er, the sky is grow - ing dark;

He is Here

Words and Music by
KIRK TALLEY
Arranged by Marty Parks

With Reverence ♩ = ca. 72

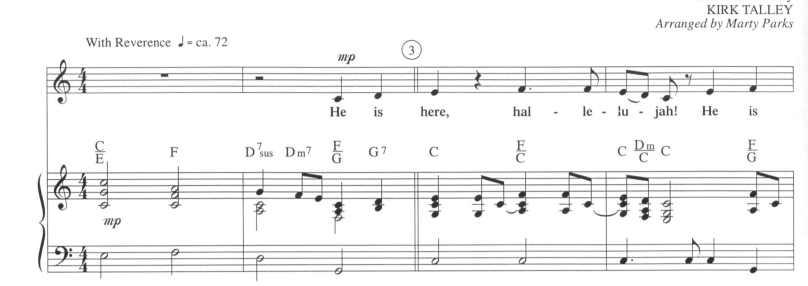

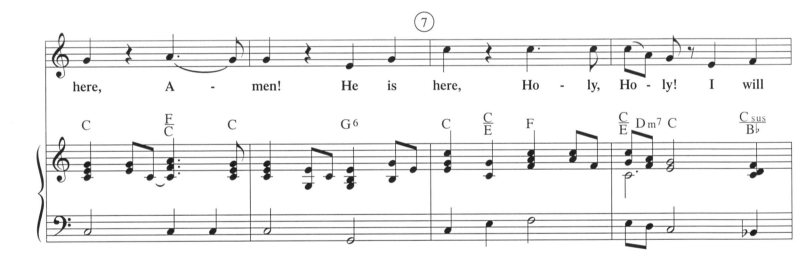

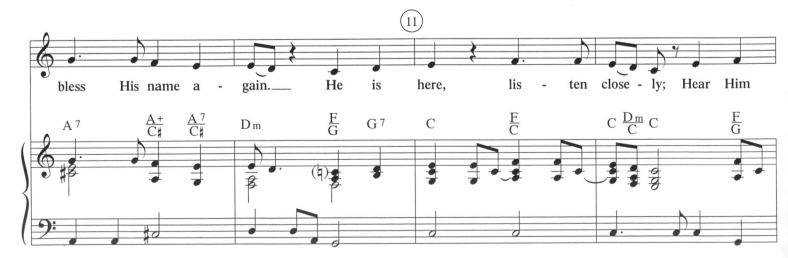

call - ing out___ your name. He is here, you can touch Him; You will

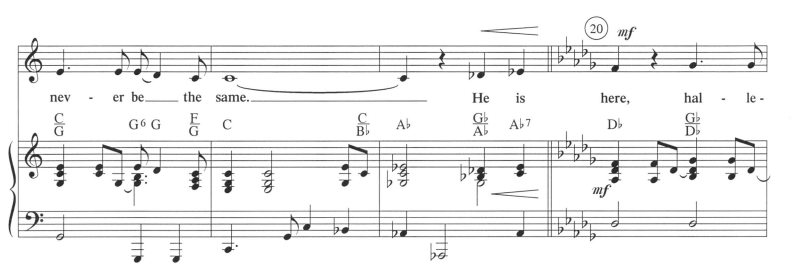

nev - er be___ the same.___ He is here, hal - le -

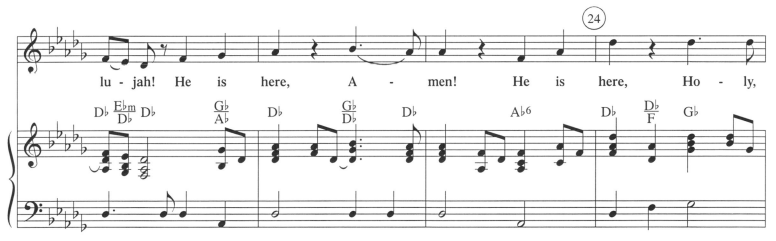

lu - jah! He is here, A - men! He is here, Ho - ly,

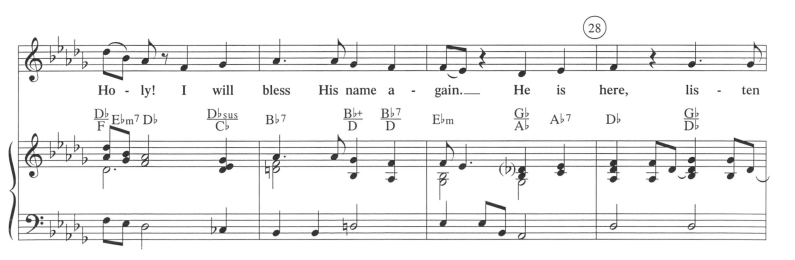

Ho - ly! I will bless His name a - gain.___ He is here, lis - ten

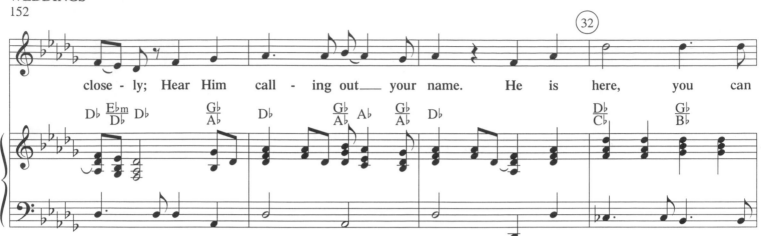

close - ly; Hear Him call - ing out___ your name. He is here, you can

touch Him; You will nev - er be___ the same.___

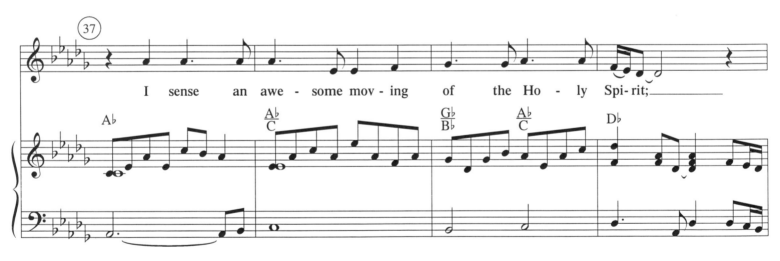

I sense an awe - some mov - ing of the Ho - ly Spi - rit;___

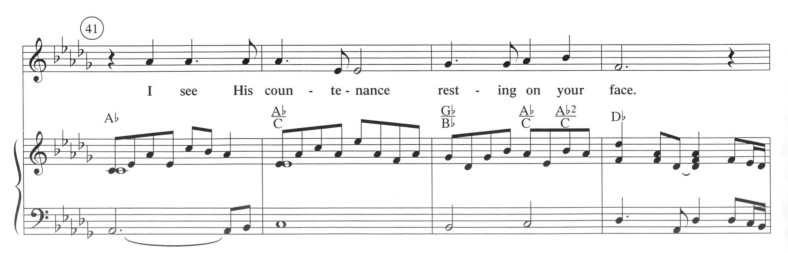

I see His coun - te - nance rest - ing on your face.

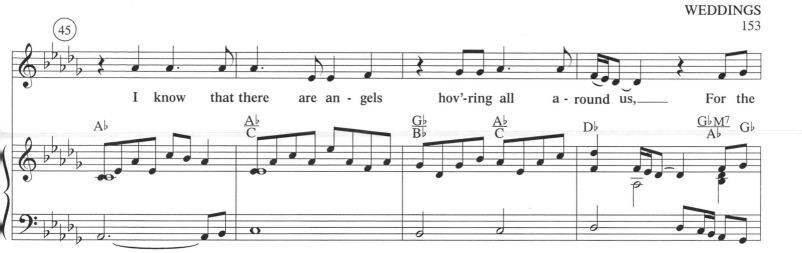

I know that there are an-gels hov'-ring all a-round us,——— For the

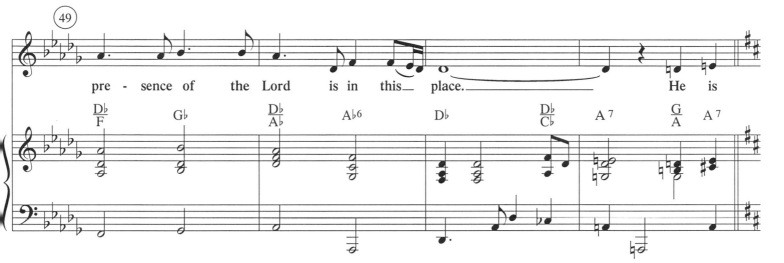

pre - sence of the Lord is in this—— place.——————————————— He is

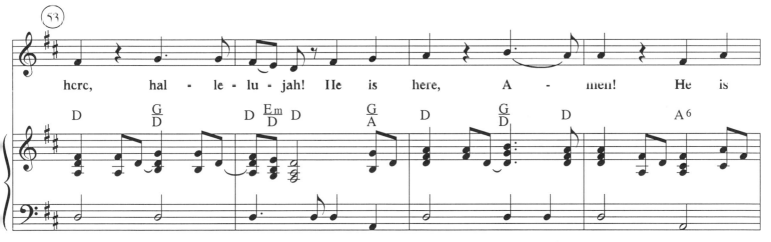

herc, hal - le - lu - jah! IIe is here, A - men! He is

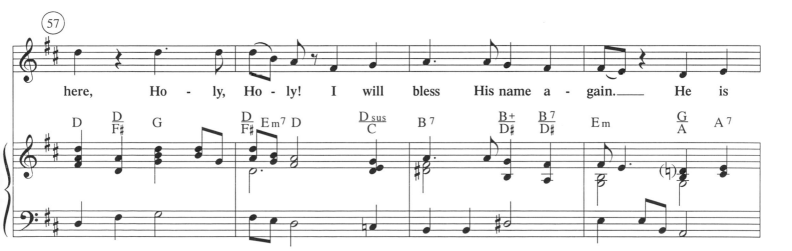

here, Ho - ly, Ho - ly! I will bless His name a - gain.—— He is

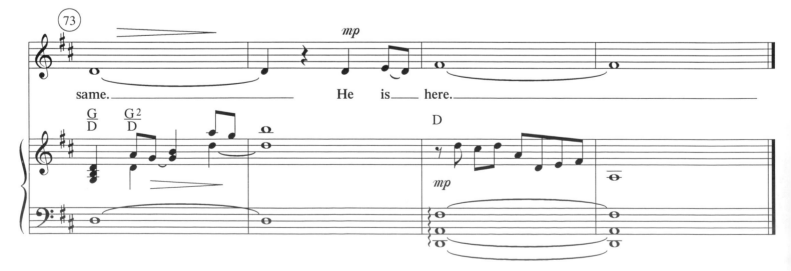

If You Could See What I See

Words and Music by
GEOFF MOORE and
STEVEN CURTIS CHAPMAN
Arranged by Marty Parks

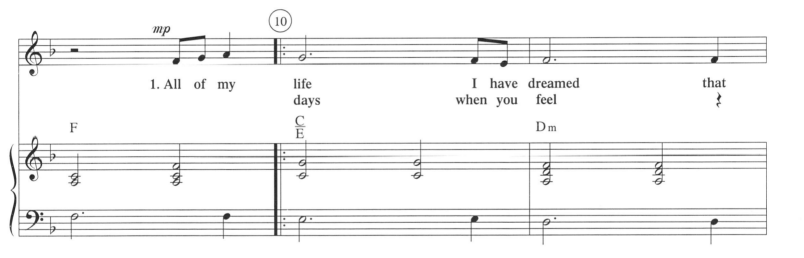

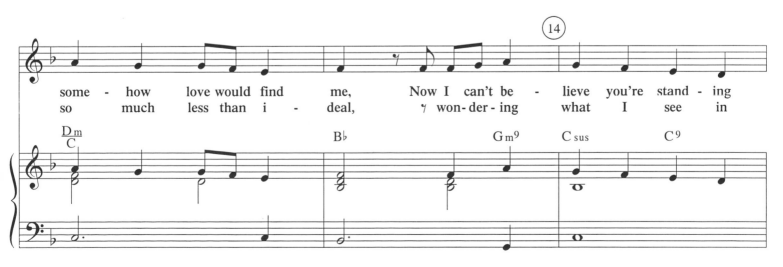

here.
you.

If beau-ty is all in the
It's all of the light and the

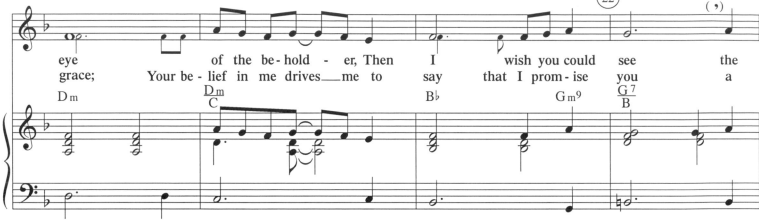

eye of the be-hold - er, Then I wish you could see the
grace; Your be-lief in me drives___me to say that I prom-ise you a

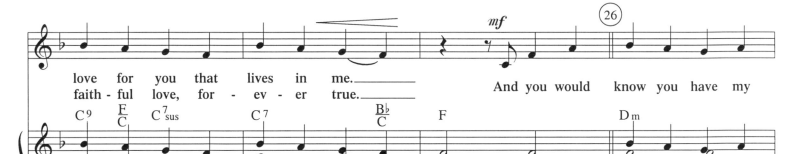

love for you that lives in me.___ And you would know you have my
faith-ful love, for - ev - er true.___

heart, If you could see what I see; That a trea-sure's what you

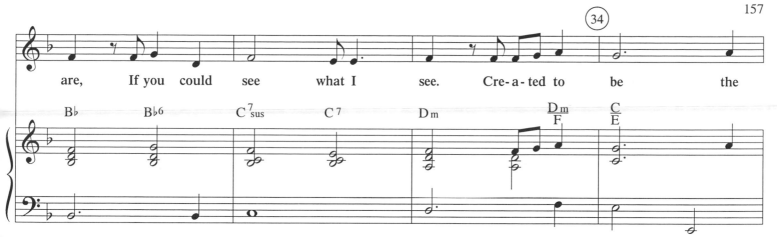

are, If you could see what I see. Cre-a-ted to be the

B♭ B♭6 C7sus C7 Dm Dm/F C/E

on-ly__ one__ for me,_____ If you could see what I

B♭ B♭M7/F B♭ B♭/A Gm7 C7

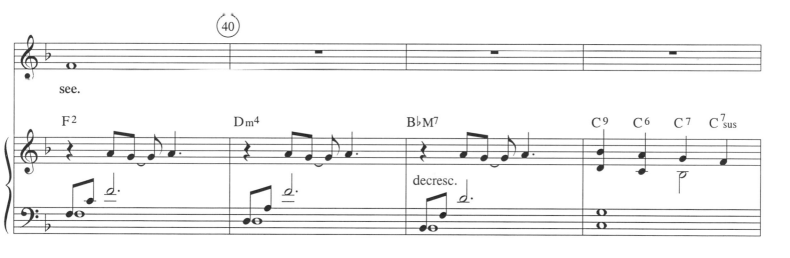

see.

F2 Dm4 B♭M7 C9 C6 C7 C7sus

decresc.

(to pg. 155, meas. 10)

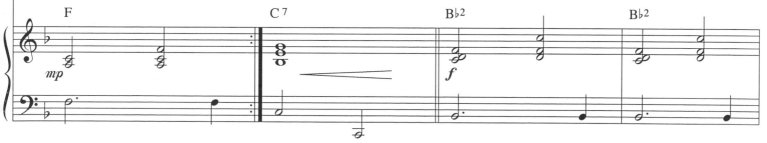

2. I know there are see, Then you'd un-der-stand_____ why I

F C7 B♭2 B♭2

mp f f

fall down on my knees,_____ And I pray my love_____ will be wor-thy of the

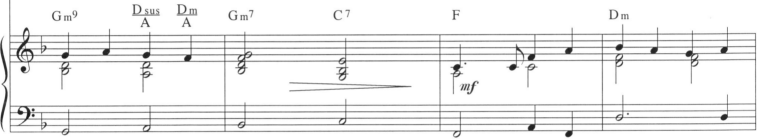

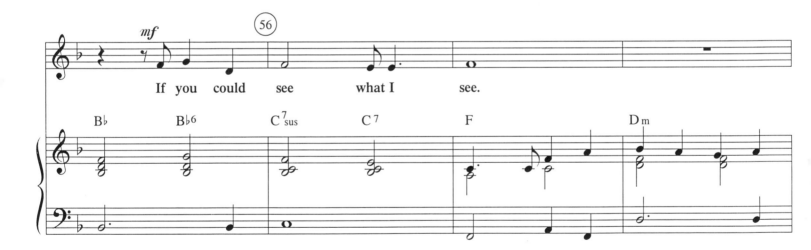

One who gave His life so our love_____ could be.

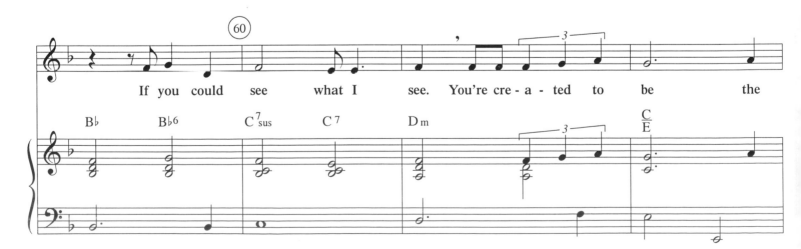

If you could see what I see.

If you could see what I see. You're cre-a-ted to be the

per - fect___ one___ for me._____ If you could see_____ what I

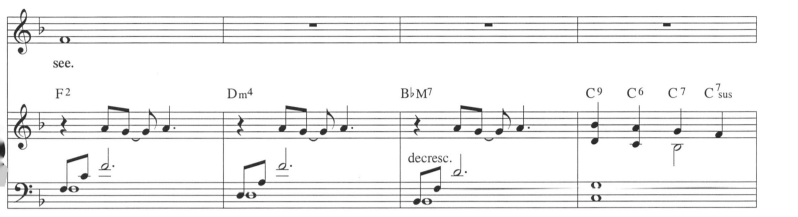

see.

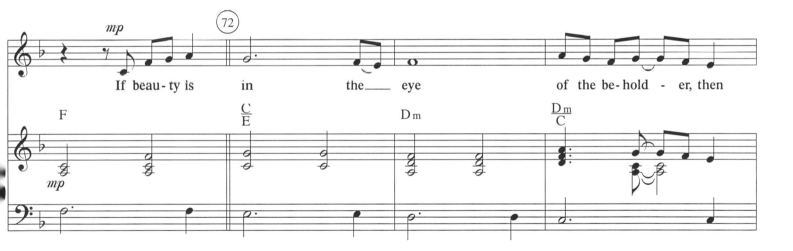

If beau - ty is in the___ eye of the be - hold - er, then

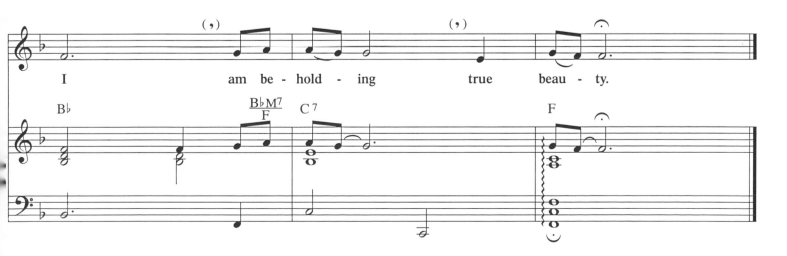

I am be - hold - ing true beau - ty.

Joy Comes In The Morning

WILLIAM J. GAITHER
and GLORIA GAITHER

WILLIAM J. GAITHER
Arranged by Marty Parks

Earnestly ♩ = ca. 80

1. If you've knelt be - side the rub - ble of an ach - ing, bro - ken heart,
(2.To in) - vest your seed of trust in God in moun - tains you can't move,

When the things you gave your life to fell a - part;_____ You're not the first to be ac -
You have risked your life on things you can - not prove;_____ But to give the things you

quaint - ed with___ sor - row, grief or pain, But the
can - not keep for___ what you can - not lose, Is the

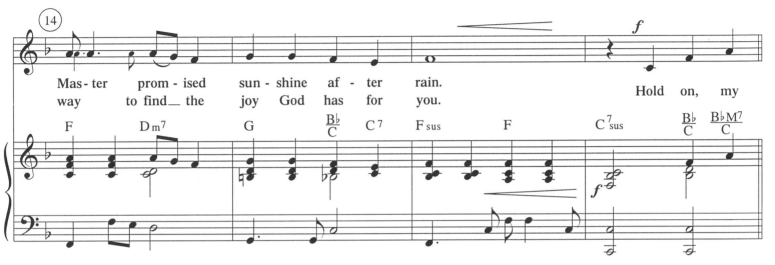

Mas - ter prom - ised sun - shine af - ter rain. Hold on, my
way to find__ the joy God has for you.

child, Joy comes in the morn - ing!

Weep - ing on - ly lasts for the night. Hold on, my

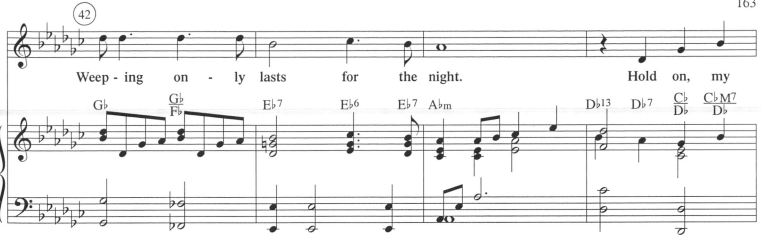

Weep - ing on - ly lasts for the night. Hold on, my

child, Joy comes in the morn - ing! The

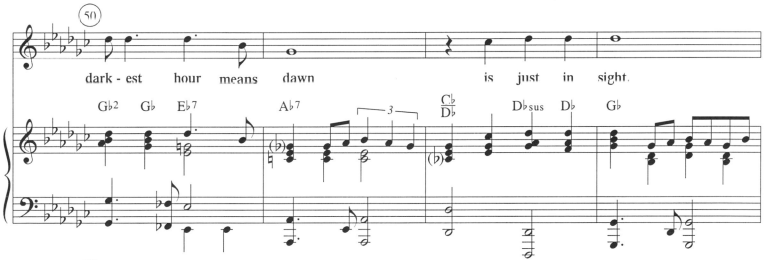

dark - est hour means dawn is just in sight.

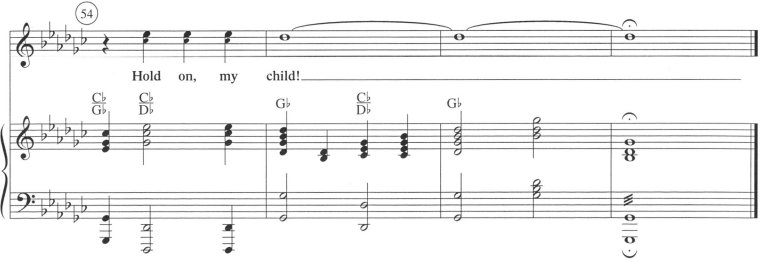

Hold on, my child!

All Your Anxiety

Words and Music by
EDWARD HENRY JOY
Arranged by Marty Parks

With Assurance ♩ = ca. 66

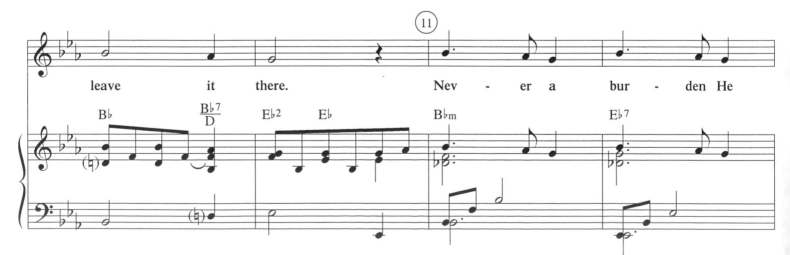

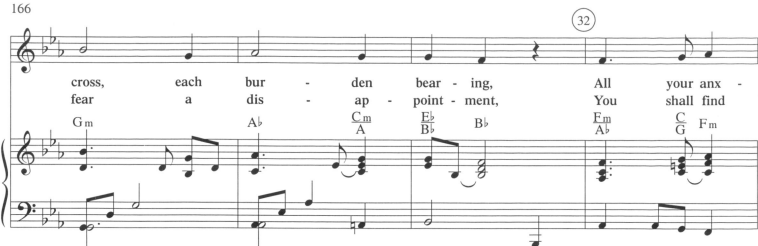

cross,   each   bur - den   bear - ing,   All   your anx -
fear   a   dis - ap - point - ment,   You   shall find

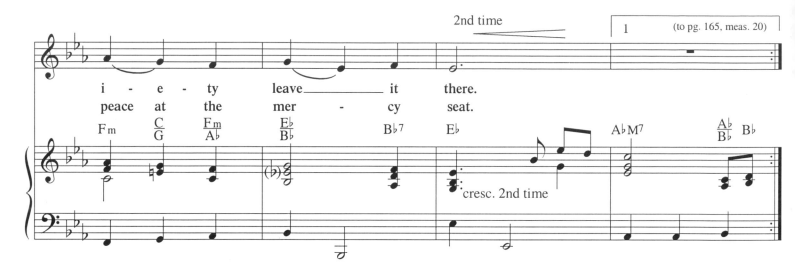

2nd time   1 (to pg. 165, meas. 20)

i - e - ty   leave   it   there.
peace   at   the   mer - cy   seat.

cresc. 2nd time

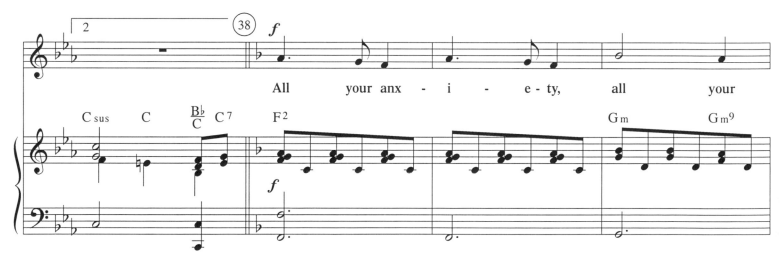

2   38   *f*

All   your anx - i - e - ty,   all   your

42

care,   Bring   to the   mer - cy seat,   leave   it

there. Nev - er a bur - den He can - not

bear, Nev - er a friend like

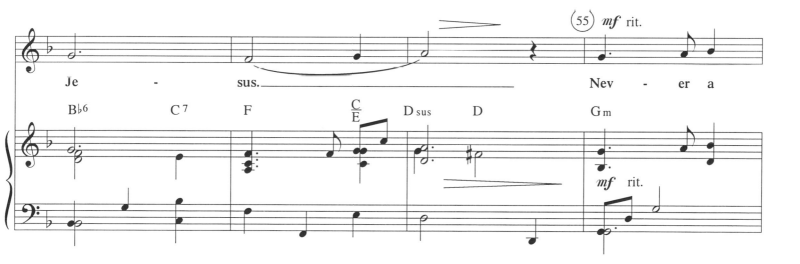

Je - sus. Nev - er a

friend like Je - sus.

He Giveth More Grace

ANNIE JOHNSTON FLINT

HUBERT MITCHELL
Arranged by Marty Parks

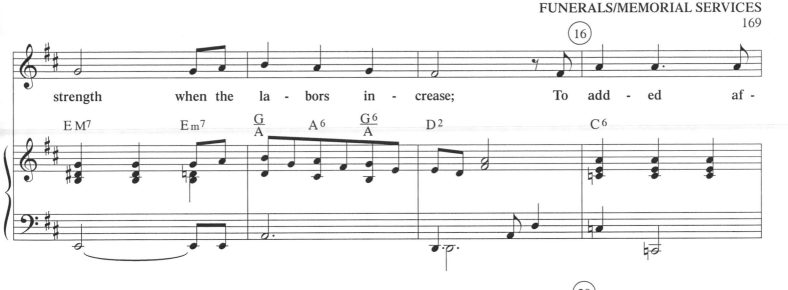

strength when the la - bors in - crease; To add - ed af -

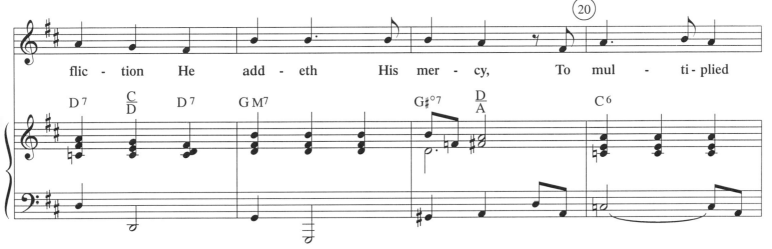

flic - tion He add - eth His mer - cy, To mul - ti - plied

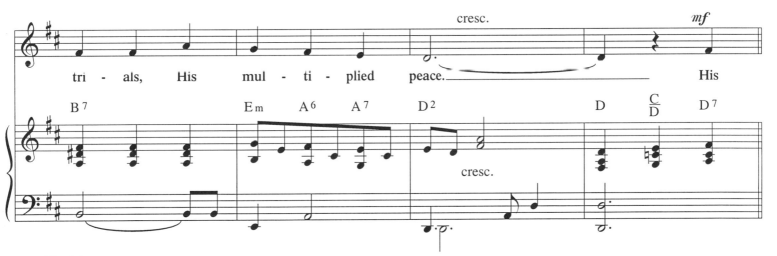

tri - als, His mul - ti - plied peace._____ His

love has no lim - it,_____ His grace has no

Lead Me Gently Home, Father

Words and Music by
WILL L. THOMPSON
Arranged by Marty Parks

With warmth ♩ = ca. 68

1. Lead me gent-ly home, Fa-ther,
2. Lead me gent-ly home, Fa-ther,

Lead me gent-ly home,
Lead me gent-ly home,

When life's toils are
In temp-ta-tion's

end-ed and part-ing days have come;
hour, Fa-ther, When sore tri-als come;

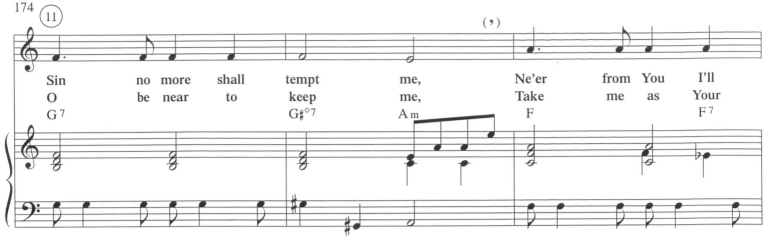

Sin no more shall tempt me, Ne'er from You I'll
O be near to keep me, Take me as Your

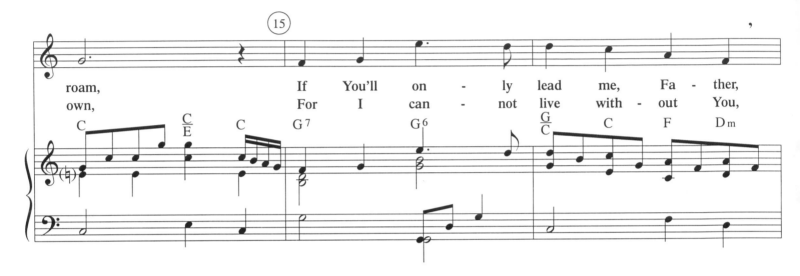

roam, If You'll on - ly lead me, Fa - ther,
own, For I can - not live with - out You,

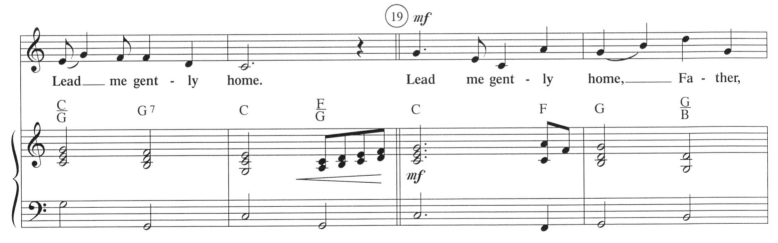

Lead___ me gent - ly home. Lead me gent - ly home,___ Fa - ther,

Lead me gent - ly home; Lest I fall up -

Blessed Are

Words and Music by
WAYNE WATSON
Arranged by Marty Parks

(to pg. 176, meas. 5)

Speak His Name

Words and Music by
MOSIE LISTER
Arranged by Marty Parks

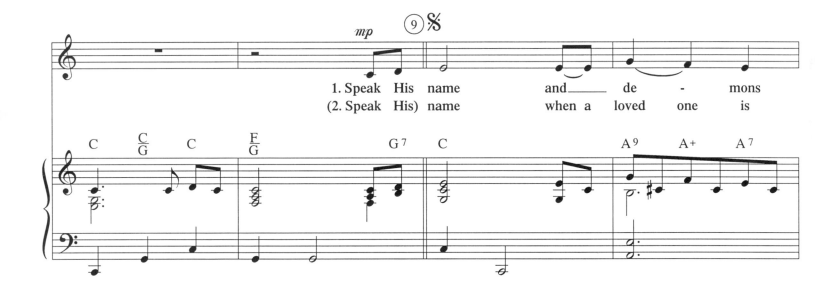

1. Speak His name and de - mons
(2. Speak His) name when a loved one is

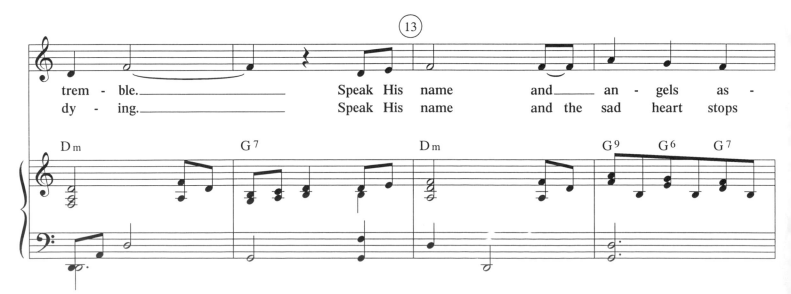

trem - ble. Speak His name and an - gels as -
dy - ing. Speak His name and the sad heart stops

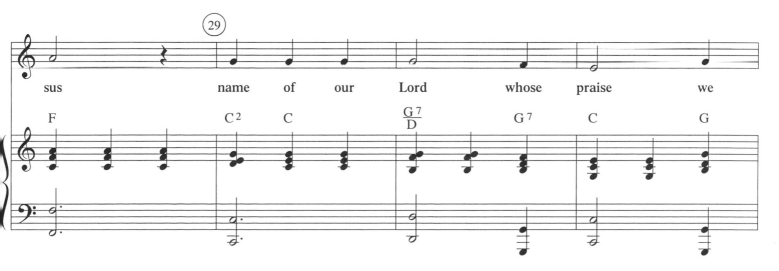

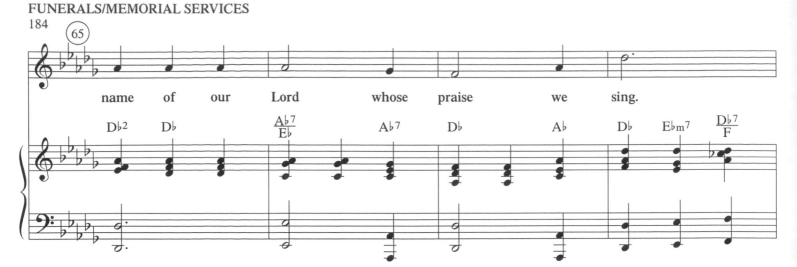

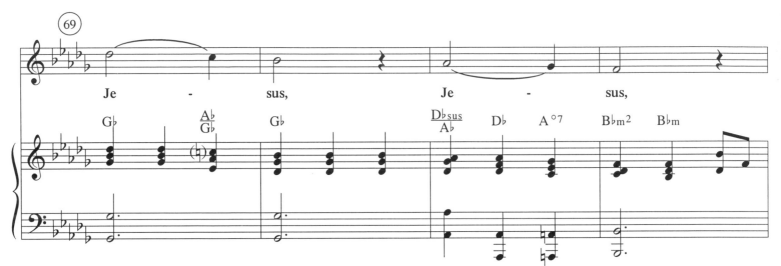

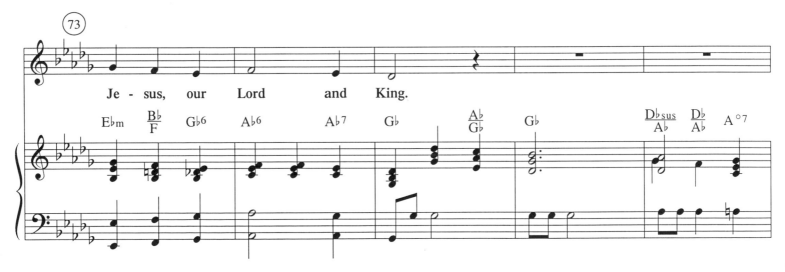

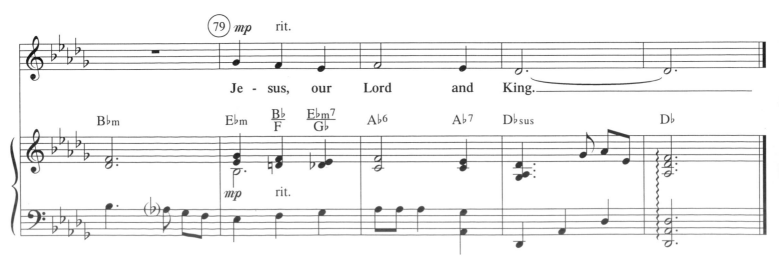

The Healer

Words and Music by
LOIS IRWIN
Arranged by Marty Parks

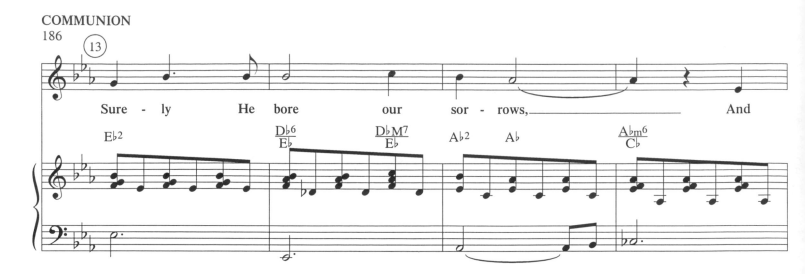

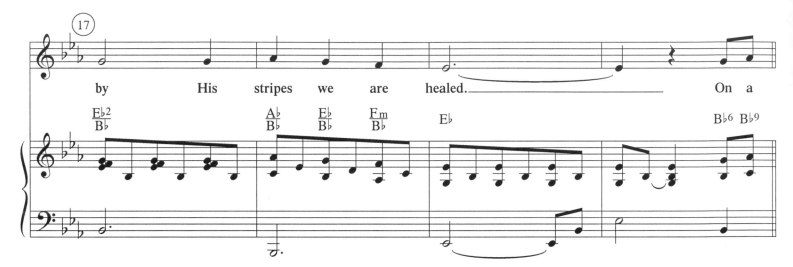

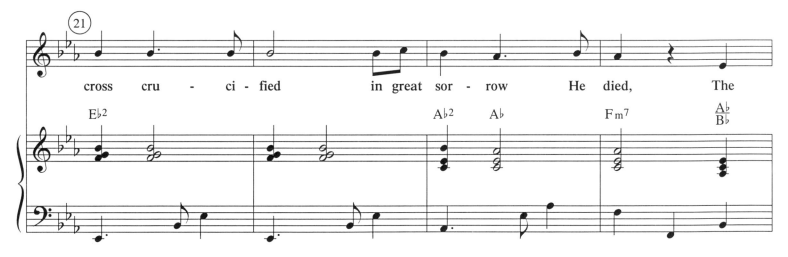

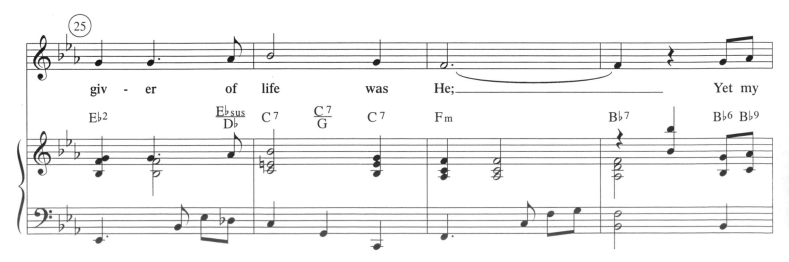

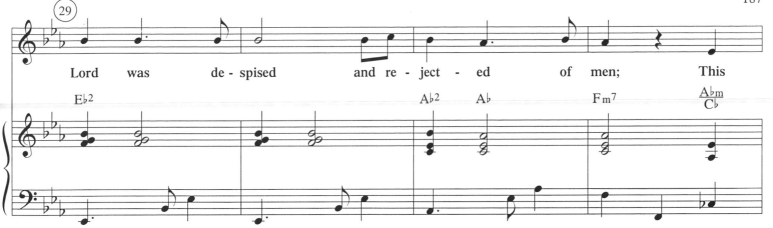

Lord was de - spised and re - ject - ed of men; This

Je - sus of Cal - va - ry. Yet, He has

healed my sick soul, made me to - tal - ly whole, And

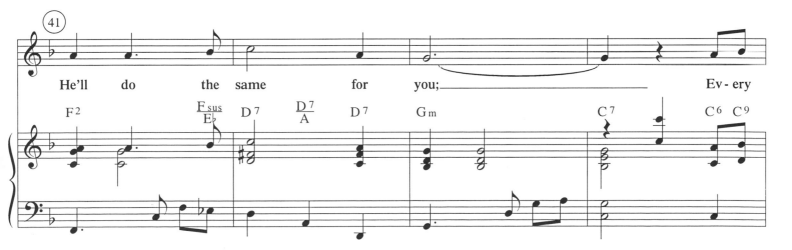

He'll do the same for you; Ev - ery

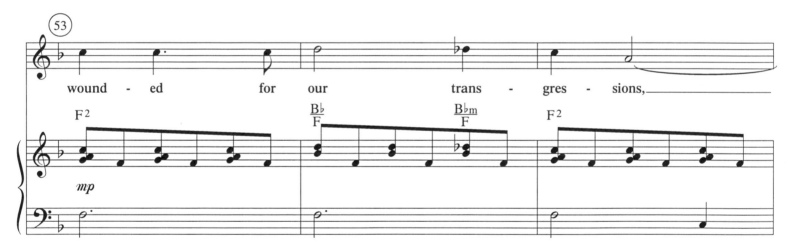

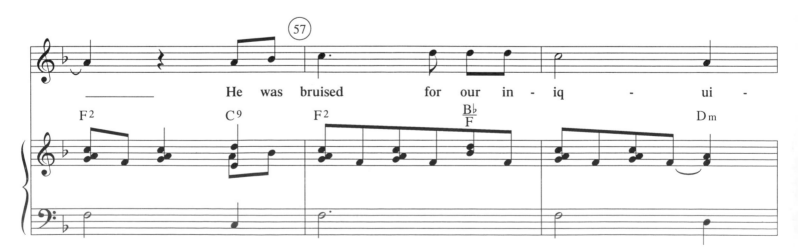

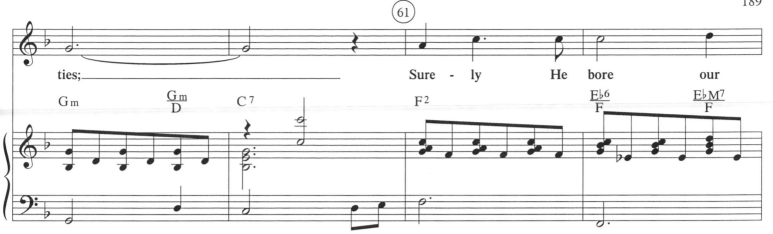

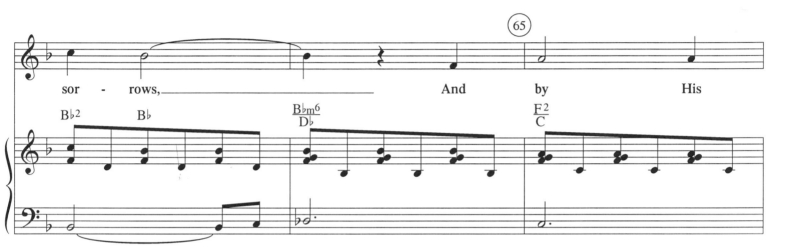

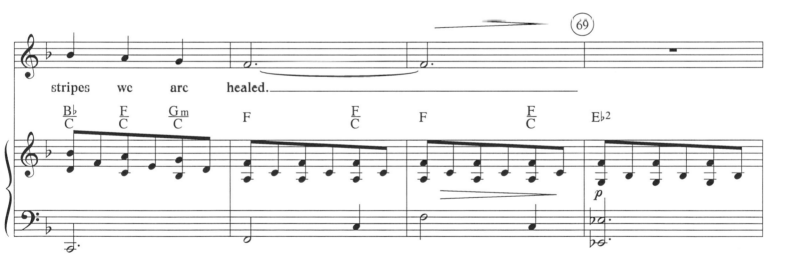

Remember the Lord

Words and Music by
DICK and MELODIE TUNNEY
Arranged by Marty Parks

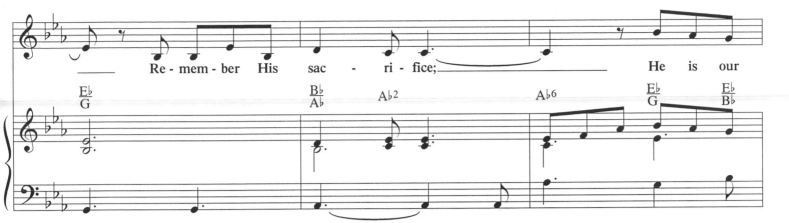

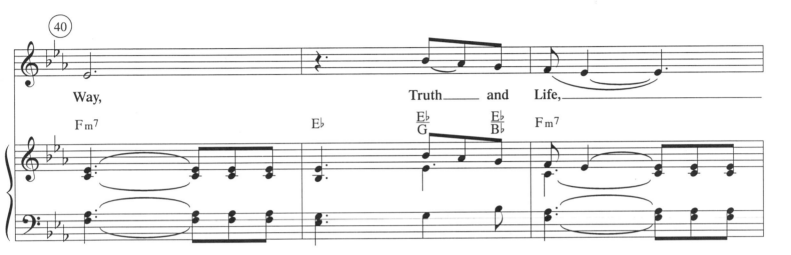

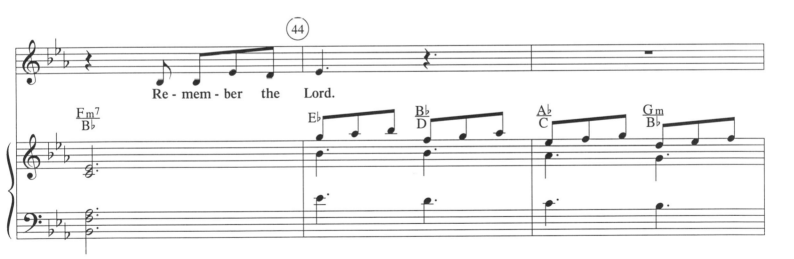

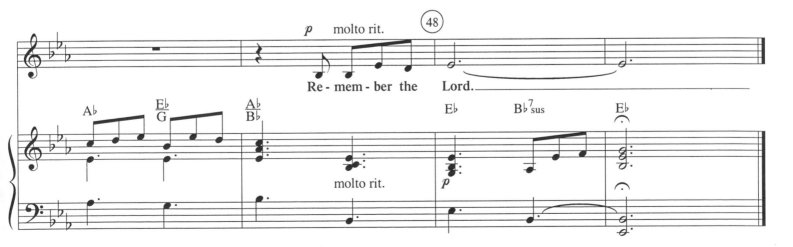

Come Just as You Are

Words and Music by
JOSEPH SABOLICK
Arranged by Marty Parks

Lyrics:
Come just as you are; Hear the Spir - it's call.
Come just as you are; Come and see,

come, re - ceive; Come and live for - ev - er.

Come just as you are; Hear the Spir - it's call.

Come just as you are; Come and see,

come, re - ceive; Come and live for - ev - er.

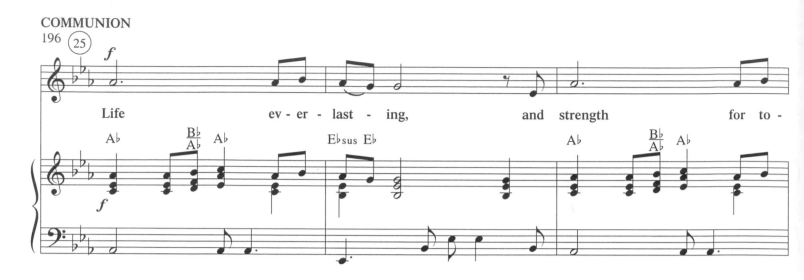

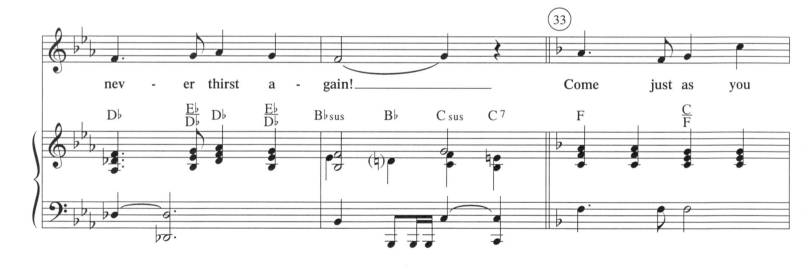

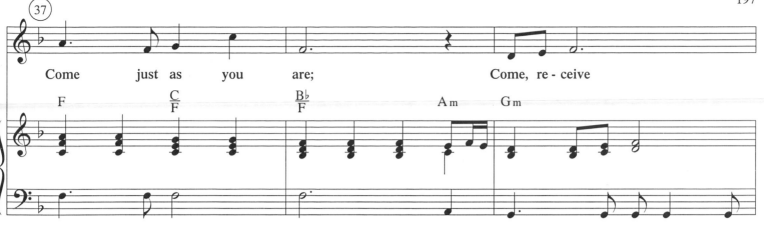

Come just as you are; Come, re - ceive

Christ, the King; Come and live for - ev - er -

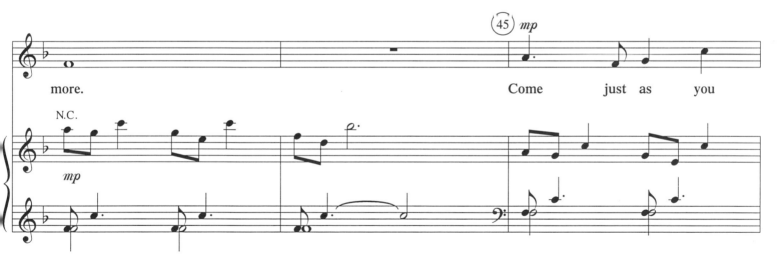

more. Come just as you

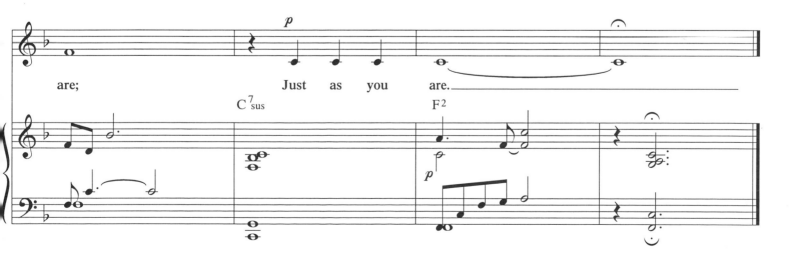

are; Just as you are.

In Remembrance of Me

Words and Music by
CHERI KEAGGY
Arranged by Marty Parks

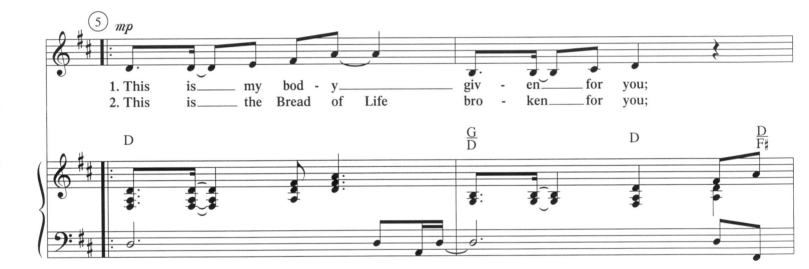

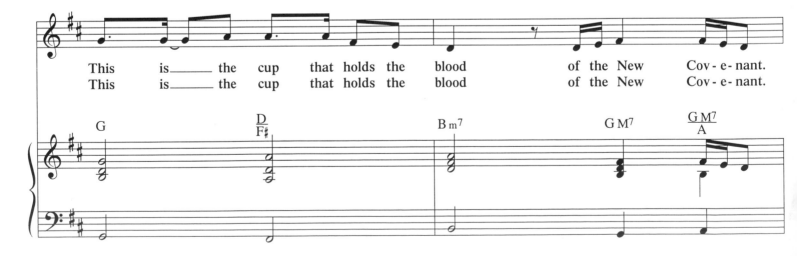

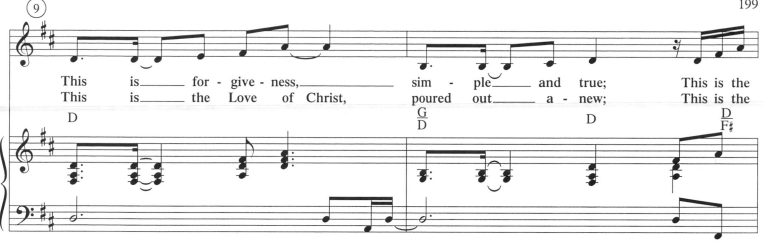

This is_____ for - give - ness,_____ sim - ple_____ and true; This is the
This is_____ the Love of Christ, poured out_____ a - new; This is the

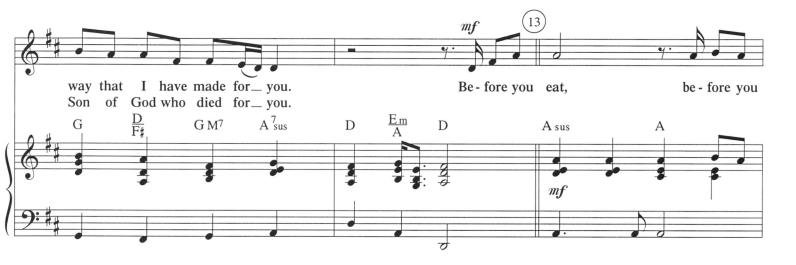

way that I have made for__ you. Be - fore you eat, be - fore you
Son of God who died for__ you.

drink, _____ Take a long look__ in - side,_____ and tell me what you see.

He said, "Do this_____ in re - mem - brance__ of Me.

See Them Come

KEN BIBLE

MARTY PARKS
Arranged by Marty Parks

flood - ing ev - ery thirst - y___ soul and mak - ing all___ things new.

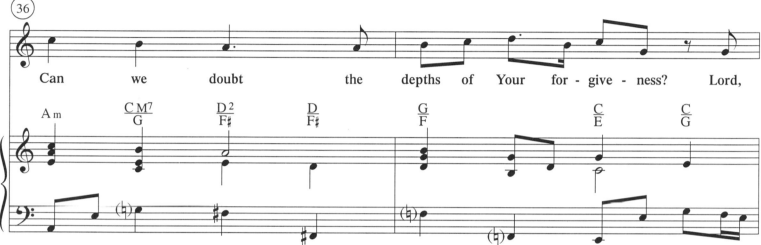

Can we doubt the depths of Your for - give - ness? Lord,

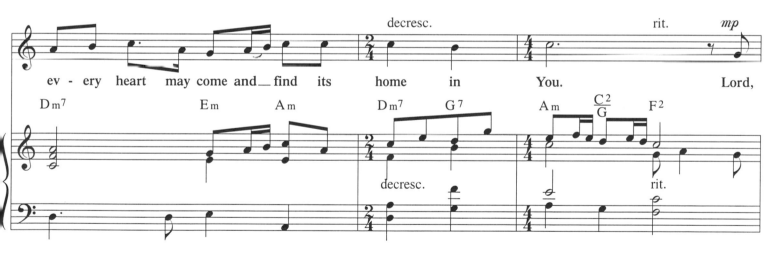

ev - ery heart may come and___ find its home in You. Lord,

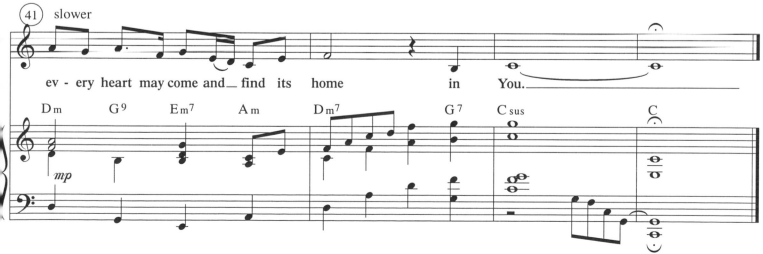

ev - ery heart may come and___ find its home in You.___

Jesus, Our Lord and King

Anonymous
Alt. by MARTY PARKS

ROBERT JACKSON
Arranged by Marty Parks

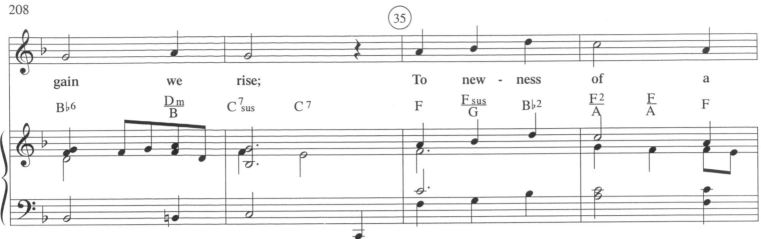

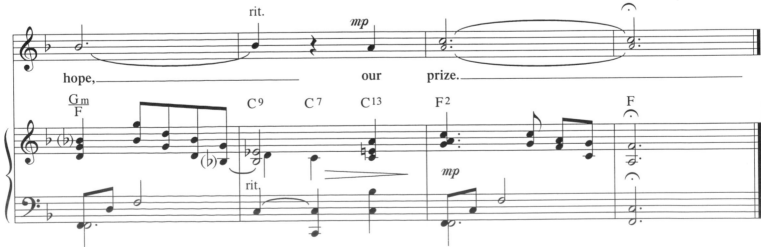

Where the Spirit of the Lord Is

Words and Music by
STEPHEN R. ADAMS
Arranged by Marty Parks

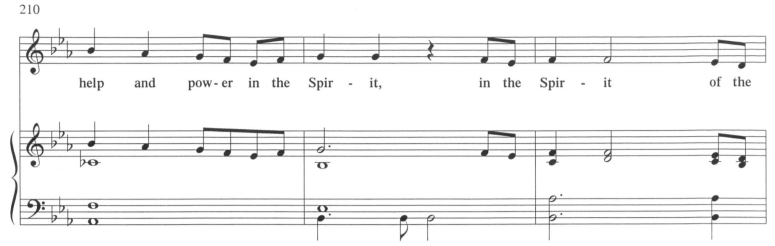

help and pow-er in the Spir - it, in the Spir - it of the

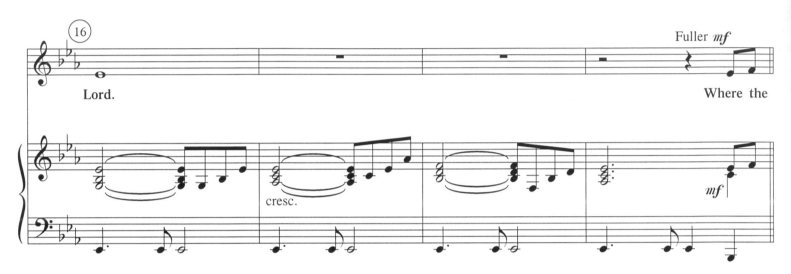

Lord. Fuller *mf* Where the

cresc. *mf*

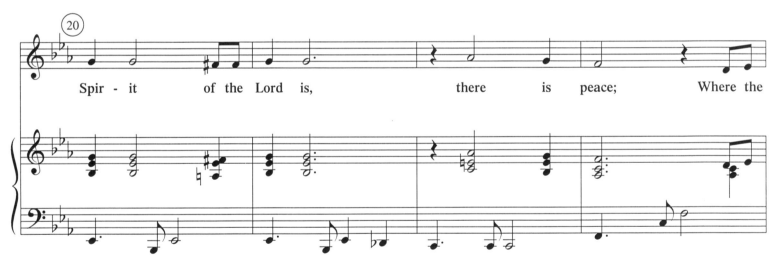

Spir - it of the Lord is, there is peace; Where the

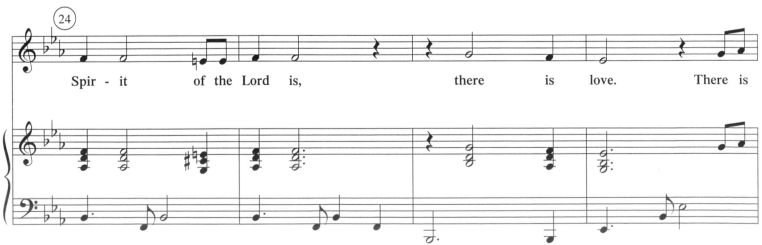

Spir - it of the Lord is, there is love. There is

com - fort   in life's dark - est hour.___ There is   light   and   life;   there is

help   and   pow-er in the Spir - it,   in the Spir - it,

In the Spir - it   of   the   Lord.___

Welcome, Welcome

LELIA N. MORRIS
and MARTY PARKS

DANIEL READ
Arranged by Marty Parks

*Verse 1 by Lelia N. Morris; verse 2 & 3 by Marty Parks

Come in pow'r and fill this tem - ple;
Look - ing to Your eyes of mer - cy;
We lift up our hearts, be - liev - ing

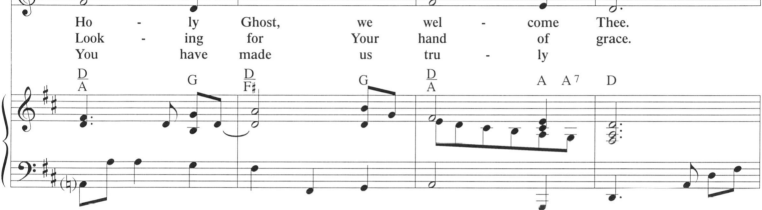

Ho - ly Ghost, we wel - come Thee.
Look - ing for Your hand of grace.
You have made us tru - ly

(to pg. 212, meas. 5)

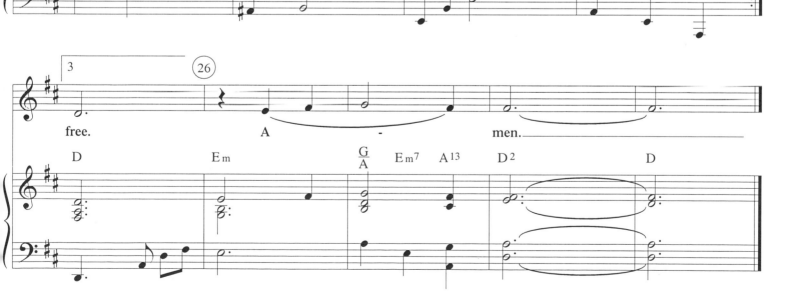

free. A - men.

I Will Be Christ to You

Words and Music by
MARTY PARKS
Arranged by Marty Parks

Expressively ♩ = ca.69

All a-lone, dy-ing in-side,___ Need-ing a com-fort,

need-ing a guide;_____ Wound-ed bro-ther, bro-ken sis - ter,

In the name of Je - sus take my hand.

I will be Christ to you, I will be Christ to you;

I'll be His hands to do what I can, Be -

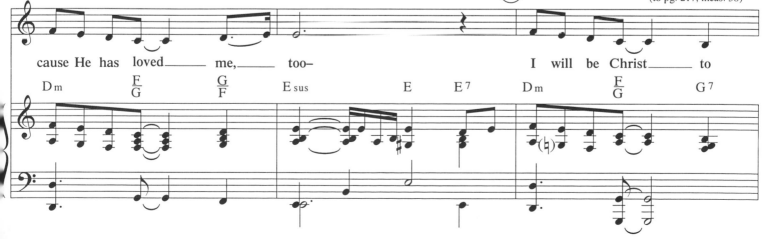

cause He has loved me, too— I will be Christ to

2nd time to Coda
(to pg. 217, meas. 38)

CODA

you. It's not my might or my pow - er,

It's not the strength__ of what I am;

But thro' God's love and His mer - cy,

And thro' the blood of the Lamb!___

I will be Christ_____ to you,_____ I will be Christ_____ to you;_____

_____ I'll be His hands_____ to do what I can,_____ Be-

cause He has loved_____ me,_____ too— I will be Christ_____ to

you._____ I'll be His hands_____ to

do what I can,_____ Be - cause He has loved_____ me,_____

too_____

I will be Christ_____ to

you._____

decresc.   rit.

rit.   *sub. mf*   *mp*

Hymn of Fellowship

JOHN OXENHAM, JOHN FAWCETT
and TIMOTHY DWIGHT

MARTY PARKS
Arranged by Marty Parks

1. In Christ there is no east or west, no south or north;_____ But one great fel-low-ship of love thro'-

2. Blest be the tie that binds our hearts in Chris-tian love;_____ The fel-low-ship of kin-dred minds is_____

(to pg. 220, meas. 5)

Here I Am, Lord

DANIEL L. SCHUTTE
Based on Isaiah 6:8

DANIEL L. SCHUTTE
Arranged by Marty Parks

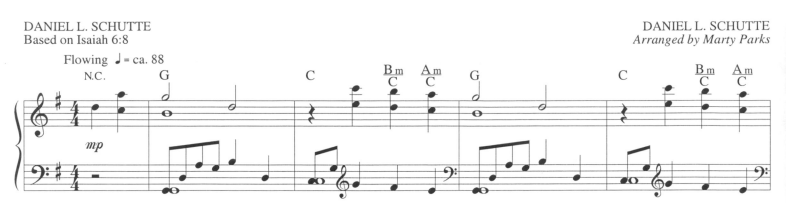

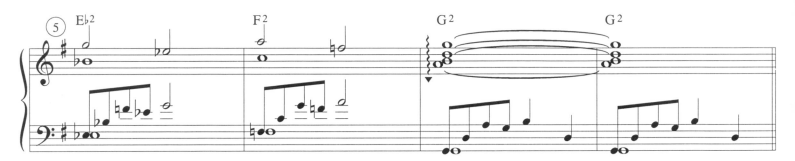

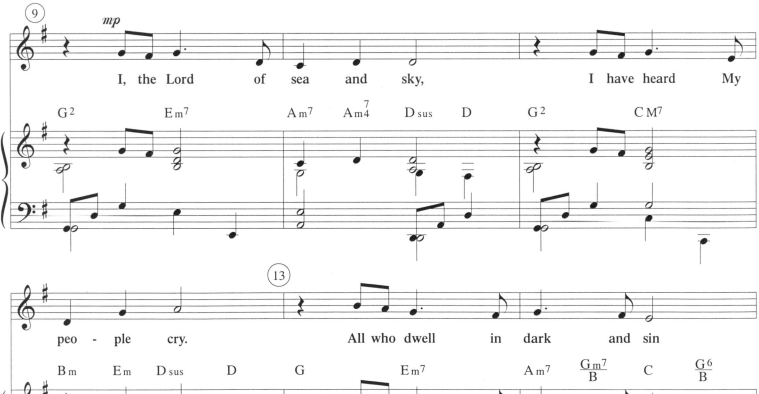

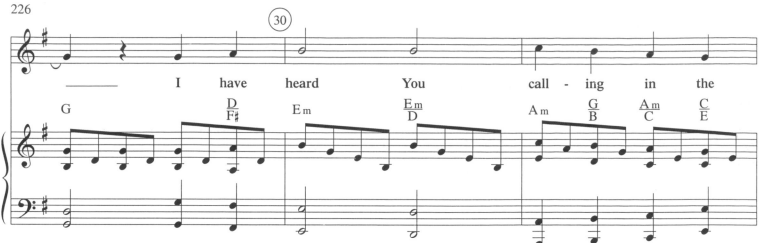

I have heard You call - ing in the

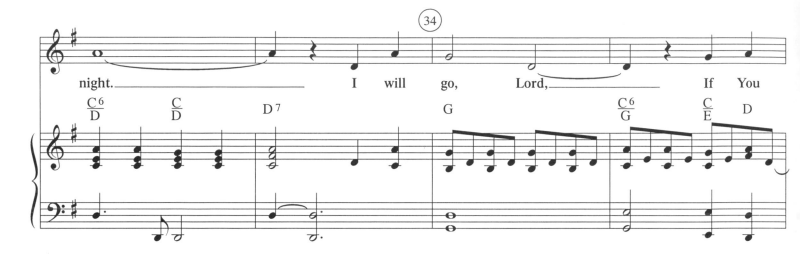

night. I will go, Lord, If You

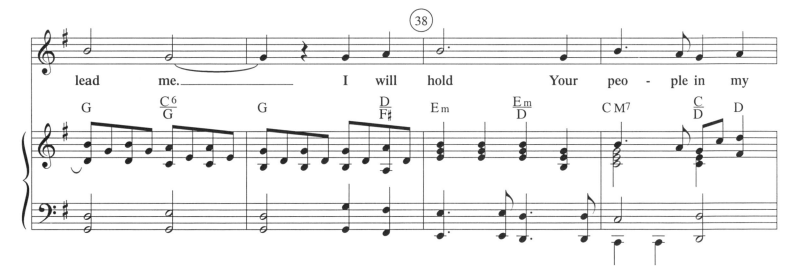

lead me. I will hold Your peo - ple in my

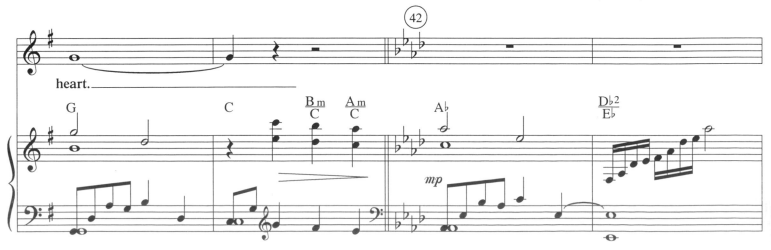

heart.

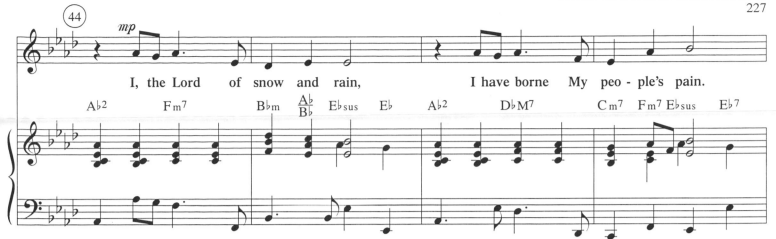

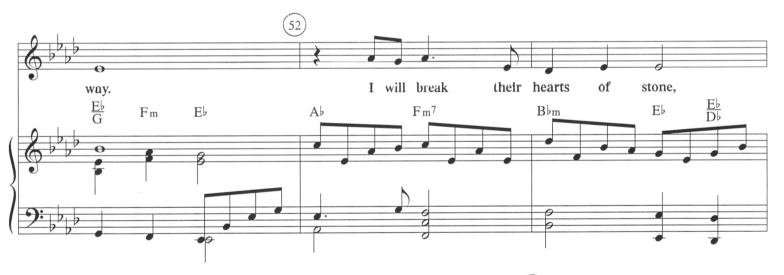

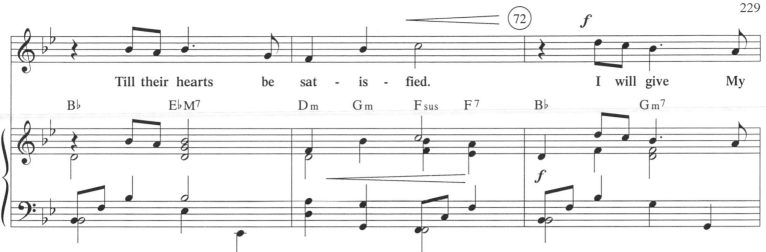

Till their hearts be sat - is - fied. I will give My

life to them. Whom shall I send? Here I

am, Lord! Is it I, Lord?

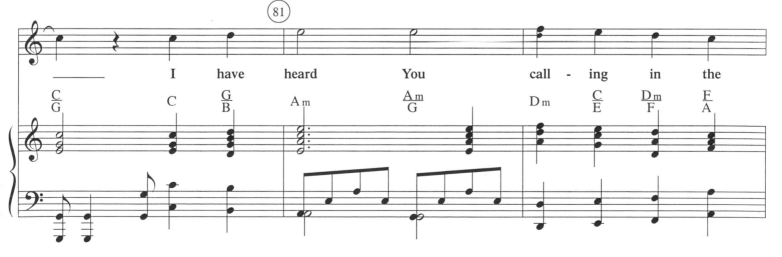

I have heard You call - ing in the

I WILL SING OF MY REDEEMER
Topical Index

I WILL SING OF MY REDEEMER
Alphabetical Index